4.95

Personal Responsibility

Think Now

Think Now is a brand new series of stimulating and accessible books examining key contemporary social issues from a philosophical perspective. Written by experts in philosophy, these books offer sophisticated and provocative yet engaging writing on political and cultural themes of genuine concern to the educated reader.

Available now:

The Ethics of Climate Change, James Garvey
War and Ethics, Nicholas Fotion
Terrorism, Nicholas Fotion, Boris Kashnikov and Joanne K. Lekea

Forthcoming:

Beyond Animal Rights, Tony Milligan
Digital Justice, Justine Johnstone
Identity Crisis, Jeremy Stangroom
Just Warriors, Inc., Deane-Peter Baker
Nanoethics, Dónal P. O'Mathuna
The Ethics of Metropolitan Growth, Robert Kirkman
The Ethics of Trade and Aid, Christopher D. Wraight

Series Editors:

James Garvey is Secretary of The Royal Institute of Philosophy and author of *The Twenty Greatest Philosophy Books* (Continuum).
Jeremy Stangroom is co-editor, with Julian Baggini, of *The Philosophers' Magazine* and co-author of *Why Truth Matters, What Philosophers Think* and *Great Thinkers A–Z* (all Continuum).

Personal Responsibility

Why It Matters

Alexander Brown

continuum

Continuum International Publishing Group
The Tower Building
11 York Road
London SE1 7NX

80 Maiden Lane
Suite 704
New York NY 10038

www.continuumbooks.com

British Library Cataloguing-in-Publication Data
A catalogue record for this book is available from the British Library.

ISBN: HB: 978-1-8470-6398-4
        PB: 978-1-8470-6399-1

Library of Congress Cataloging-in-Publication Data
Brown, Alexander, 1974 Dec. 27-
    Personal responsibility : why it matters / Alexander Brown.
        p. cm.
    Includes bibliographical references and index.
    ISBN-13: 978-1-84706-398-4 (HB : alk. paper)
    ISBN-10: 1-84706-398-5 (HB : alk. paper)
    ISBN-13: 978-1-84706-399-1 (pbk. : alk. paper)
    ISBN-10: 1-84706-399-3 (pbk. : alk. paper)   1. Responsibility.   I. Title.

    BJ1451.B76 2009
    170--dc22

                                                      2009006847

Typeset by Servis Filmsetting Ltd, Stockport, Cheshire
Printed and bound by the MPG Books Group, UK

for Tasha

Contents

Acknowledgements

I wish to start by thanking Jonathan Wolff, who supervised my PhD within the Department of Philosophy at University College London with tremendous insight and patience. During the long and perilous course of my thinking and writing on personal responsibility I have also benefited greatly from discussions and correspondence with Richard Arneson, David Miller, Anne Phillips and Alex Voorhoeve.

I am indebted to Tania Burchardt, Jennifer van Heerde, Martin McIvor, Harald Schmidt, Carrie Shirtz, Nicole Vincent and James Wilson whose comments and suggestions on earlier drafts of the book greatly improved the finished product. I would also like to thank Lucy Woodbine for her research assistance on Chapter 7.

I pay tribute to the two series editors, James Garvey and Jeremy Stangroom, for their help and support in bringing the book to fruition. Credit must also go to Sophie Cox for her sensitive copy-editing.

Finally, I am grateful to *Journal of Applied Philosophy* for permitting me to use revised material from 'If We Value Individual Responsibility, Which Policies Should We Favour?', *Journal of Applied Philosophy* 22 (2005), 23–44.

1   Introduction

On a cold, frosty day the ants began dragging out some of the grain they had stored during the summer and began drying it. A grasshopper, half-dead with hunger, came by and asked the ants for a morsel to save his life.

'What did you do this past summer?' responded the ants.

'Oh,' said the grasshopper, 'I kept myself busy by singing all day long and all night.'

'Well then,' remarked the ants, as they laughed and shut their storehouse, 'since you kept yourself busy by singing all summer, you can do the same by dancing all winter.'

Aesop

The subject of this book is personal responsibility. This is, of course, an ethical issue, but it is also very much a political issue. What, if anything, should the state, acting on behalf of society, do to help people who can work but who nevertheless prefer to remain idle, who suffer from diseases caused by unhealthy lifestyles, who bear children they cannot afford to care for, who develop alcohol or drug addictions which ruin their lives, or who cultivate tastes for the finer things in life which they fund through unmanageable credit? At the other extreme, what, if anything, should the state do about the large rewards and bonuses paid to high-flyers in the corporate world or about the gains and losses accrued by private investors who take financial gamble that other people are unwilling to take? It is widely believed individuals bear a special responsibility for the success or failure of their own lives. But what does this really mean and why does personal responsibility matter?

Much of the philosophical literature concentrates on reasons of fairness. It is argued that individuals should be held responsible for the consequences of their voluntary choices because this is the fairest thing to do. But what other reasons do we have for caring about personal responsibility besides fairness? And to what extent are existing social policies consistent with this larger constellation of reasons? Many politicians talk of the need to balance rights with responsibilities. Some make the further claim that idleness and public dependency are harmful to the welfare recipient. But what is the moral framework behind these sorts of arguments? Finally, how can we make the ethics of personal responsibility consistent with the realities of social and political life? Indeed, what kind of society do we wish to live in and how can we make that a reality?

This book investigates the nature of personal responsibility, why it matters and what, if anything, the state should do to promote it. I look at the ideas of philosophers, of course, both ancient and modern. But I also explore the thoughts of politicians, ordinary people and social policy experts. This book is not, however, an encyclopaedia of every argument for personal responsibility, every public attitude, every political perspective, every domain of social policy, every kind of policy intervention, in every society, at all times. Rather, it looks at what currently strikes this author as the most important lines of thought on the subject and then applies this thinking to some pressing issues of personal responsibility in Britain. Although I don't provide a list of answers at the end of the book, I do develop a way of arriving at such a list democratically.

Current philosophical interest in the idea of personal responsibility owes much to the work of the American philosopher Ronald Dworkin. In his two seminal articles on equality published in 1981, Dworkin appeared to uncover an important truth about equality, namely, that treating all citizens as equals does not necessarily mean that all material inequalities are unfair. On the contrary, some inequalities are rightly viewed as the responsibility of the individual. Dworkin was certainly not the first contemporary philosopher to argue against flat equality. The libertarian philosopher Robert Nozick, for example, had previously developed a powerful objection in his stirring book *Anarchy, State and Utopia*. He argued that it is false to suppose that the state has at its disposal at any given time a pool of unattached resources to distribute as it sees fit. Resources come into the world with entitlements held over them by the people who produce or manufacture them. Even John Rawls, arguably the single most important political philosopher of the twentieth century, believed that social and economic inequalities are permissible provided they are to the benefit of the worst off. Still, Dworkin's significant contribution was to insist that the ethical standing of material inequalities depends on a distinction between personal choices and brute luck. The government should aim to make the distribution of income and wealth at any given time sensitive to people's personal choices but not sensitive to their brute luck.[1]

Like most scholars, philosophers believe that there are certain things it is appropriate for them to tackle within their particular field of study as well as things they cannot reasonably be expected to do. Analytical philosophers think that rigorous analysis of political concepts such as liberty, justice, democracy and personal responsibility can contribute much to political debate. Philosophers with a more historical frame of mind, by contrast, prefer to think about where our political concepts come from and insist that political ideas don't make any sense unless one understands them in their particular historical and political context. As well as doing conceptual and historical analysis, political philosophers often set out to establish a set of normative principles to govern political societies. In this way political philosophy is also a prescriptive enterprise.[2] On the other hand, when it comes to identifying which concrete policies should be used to solve particular social problems or narrowing down the field of workable policies to a set of policies which an electorate might be attracted to, political philosophers have tended to regard these as tasks for the policy expert or social scientist.

Nevertheless, there are some contemporary political philosophers who argue that if their discipline is going to truly engage with the urgent social problems of our age – in the sense of shedding light on what we ought to do about them – then it is crucial that however much work is done in terms of clarifying political concepts and spelling out the fundamental principles of political morality, they must eventually come down from their ivory towers and provide useful guidance to policymakers.

What might this involve? One thing philosophers can do is pay more attention to public attitudes surveys. I shall pursue this line of thought more fully in Chapter 6, but for now let me simply make the point that there can be more than one rationale for philosophers looking at opinion surveys. One rationale is to discover clues to 'the truth' about social justice and the good life. For reasons to be discussed later, I am not entirely convinced that opinion surveys have any special status in this regard. I do think, however, that they can help to narrow down the range of policies that the public is likely to accept. This may be useful either in terms of developing a philosophy that is suitable for how ordinary people actually are or in terms of developing a theory of how to change ordinary people to bring them closer to how they ought to be.

A second thing philosophers can do is develop theories that are applicable in the real world. Philosophers have been very good at telling us what their theories say under ideal conditions, but when applied to the here and now their theories can be at best incomplete and at worst counter-intuitive. Suppose a philosopher tells us that it is fair to impose responsibility on persons for the consequences of their choices only if a set of morally stringent conditions have been met including equality of opportunity. What if these conditions are rarely, if ever, satisfied in the world we currently inhabit? Does that mean nobody should be held responsible? Some philosophers seem to offer little hope of answering this question because they don't say how policy-makers are supposed to transpose conditions of responsibility designed for the ideal world onto the real world.

A third thing that philosophers can do is to reflect more closely on the impact that implementing their theories and principles can have on ordinary people. An important strand of criticism of liberal egalitarian philosophy has been that it calls for investiga-tions to determine whether persons are out of work through choice or through lack of talent. The problem is that this process can have a negative impact on people's self-respect if they turn out to be untalented. I shall return to this problem in Chapter 4. There is also an issue of privacy lurking in the background here. Take the recent controversy surrounding the use of Voice Risk Analysis (VRA) technology by Harrow council in London. VRA measures 'micro-tremors' in the human voice which are purported to indicate when a speaker is delivering words under stress, such as when he or she is attempting to deceive. Voice patterns are analysed and displayed on a computer which can be observed by council workers during phone calls to benefits claim-ants. Claimants displaying abnormal results are recommended for further scrutiny and investigation, while low-risk claimants are fast-tracked. In May 2007 the Department for Work and Pensions commissioned Harrow council to undertake a year-long pilot. The council soon reported that the technology had helped to identify 126 benefit cheats in just three months, saving £110,000. Successful or not, VRA raises legitimate concerns over the erosion of civil liberties in Britain.

Now it might be countered that if criminals and terrorists are subject to phone-tapping and other surveillance measures, then why not welfare cheats? This may or may not be a good analogy. But if the technology is used to identify bogus welfare claimants, what about white collar fraudsters and super-rich tax evaders? Surely it amounts to unfair treatment to subject the poorest members of our society to investigations that are not targeted at these other sorts of people – people whose actions can cost the rest of society far more in absolute terms. I shall have plenty to say about the responsibilities of the rich in Chapter 7.

A final thing that philosophers can do is to attend to the fact that sometimes it is a good idea to make social policies a bit simpler in order to ensure that claimants understand what they can expect from the state and what is expected of them. Money is often available that is simply not taken up by claimants because of ignorance or the hassle involved. That we need simpler rules is certainly the view expressed in the 2007 Work and Pensions Select Committee report, *Benefits Simplification*. Jobcentre managers and representatives from the Citizens' Advice Bureau told the committee that simplification would reduce staff training, improve the staff's accuracy in handling cases, reduce the numbers of appeals and tribunals and decrease the amount of uncertainty and indecision among claimants, including claimants who may wish to enter the labour market but fear how this will affect their entitlements.[3]

The attempt to do some or all of the above is often classified under the heading of applied political philosophy. The present book certainly falls within this broad category. But we might just as well call it political philosophers wooing the real world.

Reading a philosophy book is not like going to the movies: philosophers prefer to give away the ending on page one rather than dragging out the suspense until the end. Since I have no pretensions to being Alfred Hitchcock, the moral of my story will be this. There are many aspects to personal responsibility and numerous reasons why it matters. Personal responsibility can matter for reasons of fairness, but it can also matter for reasons of utility, self-respect, autonomy, human flourishing, natural duty and special obligation. Consequently, different social policies can promote personal responsibility in different ways, can embody different norms and can be more or less attractive to different people depending on the values they hold dear. Political conservatives argue that holding persons responsible for their own lives will make them more likely to take personal responsibility and this is good not only for society but also for the *moral character* of the individuals concerned. Progressives believe that it is right to hold individuals responsible for the consequences of their voluntary choices because this is a basic requirement of *fairness*. Yet there are limits to these sorts of arguments which are not always recognised. If personal responsibility implies cutting off all assistance to people who have been feckless in the past, not everyone will respond in positive ways. Some individuals will continue to sink rather than swim. Perhaps this is their genuine choice. Or maybe it has got to the stage that they simply can't help themselves any more. So, if we really care about personal responsibility as a moral good, then sometimes it might be better not to impose full responsibility now so that people might be in a position to assume responsibility at a later date. Then again, once we accept the fact that personal responsibility matters for a number of different reasons and can be pursued in a number of different ways, we need a suitable method for choosing between reasonable alternatives. I defend citizens' juries as a useful tool for settling thorny issues of personal responsibility, but with the caveat that philosophers still have much to contribute in terms of clarifying the sorts of values and principles that jurors should think about, how they should think and the overall composition of the jury.

However, there are three things that I need to make clear from the start. The first is that this book is concerned with personal responsibility particularly as it relates to social policy, which is to say that it is interested not simply in how we ought to live our lives but also how the state, acting on behalf of society, ought to respond to us.

The second thing I wish to make clear is that although the term 'social policy' ranges over many different kinds of goods – social security, unemployment benefits, education, housing, healthcare, drug treatment programmes, elderly care, and so on – one thing all these goods have in common is that they are 'excludable', meaning that the state could withhold them from particular sets of individuals without incurring excessive costs. This is contrasted with non-excludable goods such as clean air or national security, where it is nigh-on impossible to offer the good to some citizens of the country and not to others. The upshot is that the government makes decisions all the time about whether or not to exclude certain sections of society from different kinds of social goods.

The third thing is that in a representative democracy voters elect politicians at periodic intervals to make decisions about the provision of social goods. Does this mean that if we as voters elect a government with generous spending proposals for lone parents (say) we cannot reasonably complain if this is what we end up with? Or if we choose instead to elect a government which is much tougher on this group, this is democracy in action and the end of the story? Not necessarily. Choosing the right social policies is a political question but it is also a question of principle. Leaving aside for a moment the issue of whether or not the majority of taxpayers are willing to support any particular group of individuals, political philosophers are interested in asking whether or not supporting that group would be the right thing to do from the perspective of political morality. Political philosophers are also interested in asking whether or not the political system ought to be reformed so that ordinary citizens have a greater say in the development and reform of government policy not merely at election time but also during a government's term in office.

However, to begin at the beginning: responsibility is a notoriously promiscuous notion. Since becoming the leader of the Conservative Party in 2005, for example, David Cameron has given a series of speeches on the subject of responsibility. He has called for nothing less than a 'revolution in responsibility' as a way of 'fixing our broken society'. His speeches contain references to various kinds of responsibility, everything from taking responsibility for our own diets to acting more responsibly as family members, neighbours, workers and citizens. He often cites the example of anti-social behaviour and argues that both parents and the wider community have a social responsibility to make it clear how people ought to behave in public.[4] While few ordinary people or even politicians bother to stop and think about the nature of personal responsibility in particular, in this book I shall attempt to do just that.

Chapter 2 explores the language of personal responsibility and tries to develop a conceptual framework for thinking about the subject. I shall outline some common conceptions of what personal responsibility means and delve more deeply into the nature of responsibility as understood by philosophers. I also enumerate some things that people might be personally responsible for and distinguish between some of the different ways in which a government might hold people personally responsible.

Chapter 3 turns to consider why personal responsibility matters from a moral point of view. Many contemporary philosophers think that personal responsibility matters for reasons to do with fairness or fair play. They claim that it is unfair for the state to force hard-working taxpayers to support people who are feckless or lazy. This is one instance of the more general Kantian intuition that says we should never treat other people purely as a means to an end but always at the same time as ends in themselves. But even among philosophers who share this Kantian intuition there are significant disagreements about what it means when applied to issues of social welfare.

Chapter 4 investigates whether or not, and how far, personal responsibility matters for reasons other than fairness. Utility, self-respect, autonomy, human flourishing, natural duty and special obligation are all considered. Once we adopt a pluralistic view of the ethical significance of personal responsibility, however we open up the possibility of value conflict. This in turn make it harder to arrive at definitive prescriptions about which socia policies best advance our concerns at any given time. Some thin that fairness always takes priority. I prefer to leave conceptu space for the possibility that sometimes fairness is not the mc important reason, all things considered. Indeed, one point that has been systematically ignored in the literature is that in some instances it may be better not to hold individuals responsible for their past choices by denying them aid now, so that they might be better able to take personal responsibility in the future.

Chapter 5 looks at the views of leading politicians on both sides of the Atlantic about the nature and importance of personal responsibility. The idea that each person bears a special responsibility for the success or failure of his or her own life has long been a preoccupation of the political right. But this idea is now championed by all major parties. From Brown to Obama politicians insist that individuals should save for the future; rely on their own hard work to satisfy their needs; adjust their personal ends to the shares of resources they can reasonably expect to receive over the course of their lives; do what they can to avoid unhealthy lifestyles. In Britain, both Labour and the Conservatives talk of the need to balance rights with responsibilities. But what does this mean and why does it matter so much? In fact, a number of British politicians have supported the idea of establishing a Bill of Rights and Responsibilities for Britain. Some legal and constitutional experts have raised concerns over the inclusion of responsibilities. Responding to these worries, I propose that if personal responsibility matters as much as politicians seem to think, then there may be a case for inserting something like the right to personal responsibility into any new Bill of Rights rather than a list of responsibilities. I also turn the spotlight on the role of politicians in all of this. In this way I try to give expression to the thought that if politicians expect ordinary people to behave more responsibly, they must begin to behave more responsibly themselves.

Chapter 6 investigates public attitudes to personal responsibility in Britain and elsewhere. I start by contrasting some very different reasons for looking into public surveys including the idea that they provide clues to the truth about the right and the good and the idea that if philosophers are going to offer helpful guidance to policymakers, then they need to pay more attention to what kinds of policies are popular among ordinary people. Turning to the evidence itself, this reveals that as compared to other countries the British are reasonably content with the current division between personal and government responsibility for social welfare. However, this general picture masks significant differences of opinion regarding different kinds of welfare claimants. People tend to take a dim view of individuals whom they perceive as having no excuse for being unemployed as compared to other groups. Differences also emerge when it comes to access to social security as compared to access to medical treatment. On average, people in Britain (and in mainland Europe) are much less in favour of penalising individuals for irresponsible behaviour in the area of health than in the area of social security.

Chapter 7 outlines some pressing issues of personal responsibility facing Britain today: the use of sanctions to force young people and the long-term jobless to take up work or training schemes; whether or not jobseekers should be excused from work requirements on grounds of conscience; the extent to which patients should bear the consequences of their own behaviour in terms of how much they must pay for healthcare and access to scarce medical resources; whether or not it is appropriate to spend large sums of taxpayers' money on drug addiction programmes; the most fitting government response to personal debt or financial losses caused by irresponsible borrowing or bad gambles; whether or not too much attention has been focused on the responsibilities of the poor ignoring the responsibilities of the rich. Here I try to set out not only the facts and figures but also the moral principles that support some policies rather than others.

Chapter 8 develops an account of how as a society we might decide what to do about these issues. I argue that even though decisions on social policy should in the final analysis be taken by elected officials and public authorities, there should be a much greater role for democratic engagement than there is at present. I proffer citizens' juries as one possible vehicle for this engagement. I also respond to potential criticisms.

The final chapter tries to pull together the various threads of argument presented in the book and to bring out its main conclusions.

2 What is Personal Responsibility?

Though we must all recognize the equal objective importance of the success of a human life, one person has a special and final responsibility for that success – the person whose life it is.

Ronald Dworkin

We use the language of personal responsibility in a variety of different ways to make subtly different points about why people find themselves in difficult situations, how they should behave and what, if anything, the rest of society should do to help them. This usage can be perplexing at times and so the purpose of this chapter is to get clearer about what we mean by 'personal responsibility'. Employing the method of conceptual analysis, I try to make progress in this direction by analysing expressions of the form 'X is personally responsible for situation S', 'X ought to take personal responsibility for S' and 'X should be held personally responsible for S'.

ORDINARY LANGUAGE

We begin with an apparently straightforward case which is actually anything but straightforward. Think about a lone parent with a four-year-old son who receives tax credits and vouchers for free childcare from the government in order to help her undertake paid employment. Thus far neither she nor the authorities have been able to force the absent father to accept his responsibilities. Although it makes perfect sense to say that she is taking responsibility for her child by making decisions about who will look after him, there is also a sense in which she is not taking personal responsibility for the day-to-day care of her child. She takes responsibility in the sense that she works for a living, but she does not take personal responsibility in the sense that she is still reliant on the state to make ends meet. So what is going on here? What is personal responsibility?

Personal responsibility can mean the responsibility assumed by a person rather than a representative. When I make it my personal responsibility to ensure that a colleague from another county has an enjoyable stay in London, for example, I make sure that I am there *in person* to show him or her a good time. Being personally responsible can also imply being solely responsible for something or someone without the help or intervention of another. If I am personally responsible for ensuring that the building in which I work is safely secured at the end of each working day, it may be that I alone assume responsibility for checking all the doors and windows. These initial observations help to explain *some* of the ways in which the lone parent does and does not exercise personal responsibility. She is not personally responsible for her child during the day, but during the evenings and weekends she is personally responsible. Moreover, she is personally responsible in the sense that she assumes responsibility for her own child without any assistance from the other biological parent. Nevertheless, she is not fully responsible because she does rely on the state for financial assistance.

Although we often speak of someone being or not being personally responsible for some other person or thing, in this book I am particularly interested in personal responsibility of the person by the person. That is, I want to concentrate on personal responsibility for one's own life or situation. Let us call this *reflexive personal responsibility*. When we say that someone is personally responsible in the reflexive sense, the word 'personally' functions in a special way: it underscores the fact that the *subject* and the *object* of responsibility are one and the same person. That is, it links the person with his or her own behaviour or situation as distinguished from the behaviour or situation of some other person or even group of persons. What could be more personal to me than how well or badly my own life goes?

From now on when I speak of personal responsibility I shall mean reflexive personal responsibility unless I state otherwise. However, I should make it clear that reflexive personal responsibility is not *purely* about the behaviour or situation of the person. We tend to think that taking personal responsibility for our own lives has something to do with not imposing burdens on other people. I think there is a lot of truth in this. So I say that reflexive personal responsibility is *directly* about the responsibility of the person by the person even though in some cases it is also *indirectly* about not imposing burdens on other people. Furthermore, in order to understand whether or not it is right to expect people to assume personal responsibility in the reflexive sense sometimes it will be necessary to understand their responsibilities to others. So I shall return to complex cases in which persons are unable to assume reflexive personal responsibility because they have personal responsibilities for the care of their children, disabled spouses or ageing parents.

More generally, the language of personal responsibility can be used to make both descriptive statements, that is, statements of fact or what purport to be statements of fact about why people find themselves in difficult situations, and to make prescriptive statements about how people ought to behave or how society should respond to people who find themselves in difficult situations S. Consider 'X is personally responsible for S' and 'X should be held personally responsible for S'. Putting these together we might want to say something of the form, 'Because X is personally responsible for S he should be held personally responsible for S'. But this sort of language can be deceptive. From the mere fact that someone is responsible for S it doesn't necessarily follow that he or she should be held responsible. We need an additional premise to justify this move. Indeed, saying that someone 'is' personally responsible for S may sometimes carry with it a covert normative element pertaining to how people ought to behave. Thus suppose I say of someone that he is unemployed because he didn't bother to look for work and that because of this it is only right that the government holds him personally responsible for his situation. Perhaps what I really mean is that he ought to have done more to seek work than he did. If so, then I must now explain why he ought to have done more and how. And I must do so without begging the question of whether or not he should be held responsible.

Can there be degrees of personal responsibility or is it all or nothing? Some people will take the view that *ultimate* responsibility for a range of things must fall on the person concerned. Even if the state has a responsibility to promote work, for example, the final responsibility for seeking employment must rest with the individual. Others will argue instead that the ultimate responsibility lies with the state. Of course, this is perfectly consistent with saying that the state may exercise its ultimate responsibility for the welfare of all citizens by promoting personal responsibility. It might be that individual citizens are better able than governments to judge what is likely to make their lives go well, and are better placed to take the necessary steps to achieve a good result. Nevertheless, this sort of justification for personal responsibility is contingent on circumstances. If the government discovers over time that the lives of some individuals are going very badly under this regime, the justification will fall away and its responsibility will kick in again, perhaps requiring a guaranteed safety-net for all.

Be that as it may, it is wrong to think that there must be *either* personal responsibility *or* collective responsibility. If the state sets up and then manages over time a national pension scheme or a system of public health insurance or a special fund to deal with severe flooding or other emergencies, this doesn't automatically reduce the amount of personal responsibility that ordinary people take for their own lives. On the contrary, collective action can be a way for large numbers of people to take personal responsibility together. Even so, collective action may impact on the degree to which we can meaningfully say that responsibility has been assumed *in person*.

A further query is whether or not the expectation of personal responsibility is more or less appropriate in different contexts. Suppose a close friend of yours asks to sleep on your sofa for a few days while he looks for a new flat. There is nothing wrong with this per se. It may even help to cement your friendship – stronger friendships often emerge from situations of adversity. Yet if he continues to sleep on your sofa for weeks on end without lifting a finger around the house and without looking for a new flat, then you have a right to question his personal responsibility. You might think that he is taking unfair advantage of you. Even so, we tend to think that this is an issue for you and your friend to deal with. You must decide what to do and you may feel that the friendship is more important than the principle. But if we ask 'What should the state do about this problem?' the answer would seem to be 'Leave it to friends to sort it out'.

Generalising from this example it is tempting to draw a distinction between the private domain (relationships between friends and family members, for example) and the public domain (the provision of social welfare, for example). It is also tempting to say that while the virtues of compassion and forgiveness are supremely important in the context of families or friendship, they are much less suitable in public life, where the government is accountable for spending taxpayers' money. It is important to recognise, however, that where we draw the distinction between public and private is itself a question of principle and is something that reasonable people may disagree about. Reasonable people will also disagree about which principles are most important in different contexts. Some people might think that holding individuals responsible for the consequences of their voluntary choices shouldn't always take priority over virtues of compassion in the public domain. Conversely, people might not refuse shelter to a friend the first time of asking, but they may think twice if he or she continues to call on their generosity repeatedly or over a long period of time. At the very least levels of compassion may diminish with weariness.

COMMON CONCEPTIONS

According to the above analysis, reflexive personal responsibility is the idea that persons bear a special responsibility for their own lives. Unsurprisingly, there are different ways of spelling out the details of this core idea. In this section I outline three common conceptions of personal responsibility, each of which is controversial in its own way.

The first conception highlights the idea of people as choice-makers. Thus it is increasingly argued that NHS patients in Britain should be given greater personal responsibility for their own health. Patient choice over hospitals is an often-cited example. The same sorts of arguments are also applied to welfare benefits for the disabled and important social services such as unemployment centres and housing associations. The basic idea is that by making choices about which social services to use, when and how, individuals exercise a kind of self-determination over their destinies that passive recipients do not. This is *personal responsibility as autonomy*.

Many people think that recipients of social benefits should assume personal responsibility not merely in the sense of choosing between different packages of social benefits but also in the sense of making every reasonable effort to pay their own way. This is *personal responsibility as self-reliance*. To be sure, those who are self-reliant characteristically internalise the costs of their actions, so there is the possibility of drawing an even deeper distinction here between actions which do and actions which do not impose burdens on other people. The wider class of cases might include people who rack up large credit card debts and file for bankruptcy, thereby externalising the costs of their actions. It will also include cases that fall under the general heading of social responsibility (or lack of), such as polluting a neighbour's garden, dropping litter in the street or vandalising public property. So from now on when I speak of self-reliance I shall have in mind the opposite of being dependent on others, where being dependent on others means continually looking to others to meet one's basic needs.[1]

Turning from people at the bottom of the income and wealth scale to people at the top, another popular conception of personal responsibility focuses on responsibility for positive outcomes. To claim that someone should be held personally responsible for a positive outcome, especially when it is linked to the exercise of talent or effort, is to claim that he or she should reap the benefits of that outcome. This is *personal responsibility as reward*. Many people find this conception of personal responsibility deeply intuitive. In a world where it can be fair to hold individuals personally responsible for the failure of their own lives, surely it is equally fair to hold individuals personally responsible for the success of their own lives. Furthermore, we tend to think that personal responsibility as reward is indispensable to economic growth. If we were to remove personal responsibility as reward, then we would remove the incentive for talented people to work hard and to invent new and evermore efficient products and services.

Each of the above conceptions has its strengths and weaknesses and may be more or less appropriate in different situations and at different times. Autonomy may seem like a valuable thing most of the time, but is it always good to have a free choice? Isn't paternalism important sometimes? Self-reliance may be attractive when there is low unemployment, but don't people need to rely on the state when times are hard? Likewise, the idea of personal responsibility as reward has come under attack in recent years amid public disquiet about 'fat cats' and 'city boys' whose rewards seem disproportionate to their efforts. These individuals may be hard workers, but are they personally responsible for all their rewards and bonuses?

It is also worth emphasising that these are all modern, secular conceptions of personal responsibility. A much older conception of personal responsibility puts the emphasis on our relationship with the Gods. Take Aesop's fable of Hercules and the Wagoner: when a farmer's wagon becomes stuck in the clay, he drops to his knees and begins to pray for Hercules to come and help him without making the least effort to move the wagon himself. Hercules responds by telling him to lay his shoulder to the wheel and reminds him that *Heaven only helps those who help themselves*. Similarly, an important part of the Christian doctrine of personal responsibility says that God gave free will to mankind so that individuals could take personal responsibility for their own actions. This is reflected in Albert Einstein's famous claim that man must cease attributing his problems to his environment and learn again to exercise his will – his personal responsibility.

Nevertheless, I think it is important to draw a distinction between personal responsibility and free will. Many philosophers use the term 'free will' to mean a quality of mind that enables people to exercise purposive control over their actions – a quality that is not itself caused by anything besides its own happening. For this to be the case the will must be *causa sui* or the cause of itself. The British philosopher, Galen Strawson, argues that *if* there is no such thing as free will, then human beings cannot be responsible for what they do or do not do. Now he doesn't mean to imply that we should stop punishing criminals, for example. Punishing criminals makes perfect sense in so far as it deters law-breaking. But he does mean to say that we should stop punishing criminals on the pretext that they deserve punishment or are in some sense morally responsible for their actions.[2] As will become apparent in Chapter 4, however, Strawson's views are controversial. A number of philosophers, in various fields of moral inquiry, maintain that it is right to regard people as responsible for their actions even if there is no such thing as free will. The reason being that most of us tend to assume that we are responsible for our actions and should be held responsible without supposing that we are the first cause of what we will.

Naturally the way in which philosophers think about responsibility frames the reasons they have for thinking that personal responsibility is important. So understanding what philosophers mean by 'responsibility' is a crucial next step in understanding why personal responsibility matters.

WHAT DO PHILOSOPHERS MEAN BY 'RESPONSIBILITY'?

Philosophers are fond of drawing distinctions and few concepts admit of more distinctions than the concept of responsibility. But to keep things simple, I shall only introduce four kinds of responsibility, which crop up in morality, law and politics.

Many of us do things or fail to do things which lead us to face consequences or outcomes that other people don't face. Smokers face an increased risk of a range of diseases; people with a healthy diet tend to be less at risk of heart attacks than fast food addicts; individuals who engage in extreme sports are more likely to seriously injure themselves than people who play ping-pong; persons who develop a taste for the finer things in life can face an existence with less preference satisfaction than people with more modest tastes; beach bums tend to have less income than accountants. These and other similar sorts of examples raise what some political philosophers like to call the question of *consequential responsibility*: 'When and how far is it right that individuals bear the disadvantages or misfortunes of their own situations themselves, and when is it right, on the contrary, that others – other members of the community in which they live, for example – relieve them from or mitigate the consequences of these disadvantages?'[3]

There is more than one way for the state to impose consequential responsibility on individuals. One is to simply stand back and do nothing. Take the case of a negligent uninsured driver lying injured at the side of the road. The state could hold him consequentially responsible for his actions by allowing hospitals not to give him emergency care. A less extreme method is to provide the care he needs but to make him pay the relevant costs. This can be done either before things turn out badly (*ex ante*) or after they turn out badly (*ex post*). The *ex ante* strategy has two main benefits. The first is that it abstracts from luck. Suppose two people take similar risks with their health, but one of them gets lucky and doesn't suffer any bad consequences. It seems fairer to require both individuals to pay up front, before any bad situations actually arise. The second benefit is that fewer people will end up in a situation where they urgently require assistance but are unable to pay for it. A system of compulsory insurance (say) means that the state can uphold the ideal of personal responsibility but at the same time ensure persons who get themselves into difficulty receive the help they need, when they need it. This second benefit, however, raises a question about the limits of state intervention. It might be better for individuals to pay the expected costs of their actions, but compulsory insurance schemes stand in need of justification, since arguably they amount to a loss of personal autonomy.[4]

Turning now to a second kind of responsibility, think about the responsibilities people have by virtue of the roles they occupy within a family, business, civil association or political community – roles such as parent, worker, union representative or citizen. These responsibilities, which can be assumed or acquired, are referred to in the literature as *role responsibilities*. Sometimes these responsibilities are assumed in a formal sense, as when people take on the role of spouse, teacher, doctor or lawyer. But this is not always the case, as when people acquire or are given the role of good citizen, good friend or good daughter by social convention. Role responsibilities can include both specific tasks and general responsibilities. So, for example, a doctor can have a specific responsibility to chase up the results of a test he or she ordered for a patient and be responsible for the general health and well-being of his or her patient, the reason for ordering the tests.[5]

Role responsibilities are always personal in one sense, since they concern things it is up to persons to do or see to it to obtain. Nonetheless, many role responsibilities involve looking after other people or property. Thus suppose for the sake of argument I have a role responsibility as a good neighbour to report suspicious activity to the police including strangers lurking around my neighbour's home while he is away on holiday. Although this is a personal responsibility in the sense that it is something I must do myself, the object of the responsibility in this case is my neighbour's home. Of course, if I am a bad neighbour, then other people on my street won't bother to keep an eye on my property. In the event that my house is burgled, there is one sense in which I have myself to blame. Other role responsibilities, by contrast, are reflexive, such as when we claim, 'The good citizen relies on his own hard work to make ends meet.' That said, arguably the reason why we assign this particular role responsibility to citizens is to ensure that they don't impose burdens on others. In other words, we judge that citizens have a role responsibility to work for a living so that others don't have to bear the cost of that life.

Reading only the philosophical literature can leave one with the impression that personal responsibility is solely to do with how the state might fairly distribute the costs of unhealthy, reckless or unproductive lifestyles. Yet social policy experts and politicians alike insist that creating a society of personal responsibility is not only about allocating the costs of bad outcomes but also about the steps that persons can and should take to avoid these outcomes in the first place. This is a third kind of responsibility and I shall refer to it in this book as *preventive responsibility*. Many preventive responsibilities can be viewed as role responsibilities, as when a patient has a role responsibility to follow doctor's orders. But not all preventive responsibilities must be role responsibilities and role responsibilities can include things that are not preventive responsibilities.

Politicians often use the language of preventive responsibility in connection with public health issues. They urge that individual citizens should take preventive responsibility for their own health by giving up smoking and by adopting healthier lifestyles more generally. Once again, promoting preventive responsibility is one way to ensure that fewer costs end up being imposed on taxpayers. But this is not the only motivation. Making efforts to look after one's own health may be deemed an appropriate way of life for people quite apart from the social costs associated with dealing with illness and disease. Of course, questions of preventive responsibility can also arise when third parties manufacture risks for the general population. Consider the tobacco industry. What responsibility does it have for making the dangers of smoking known to its customers? Did the government act reasonably when it required tobacco companies to place large warning signs, such as 'Smoking Kills', on cigarette packets?

Preventive responsibility is not limited to public health issues. Debates about the problem of personal debt are loaded with arguments about the practical steps that individuals can and should take to avoid financial problems before they arise – working hard, maintaining a steady flow of income, saving for the future, limiting financial burdens wherever possible, not building up too much credit, using birth control if one cannot afford to look after more children, and so on. It is worth emphasising again that in many of these instances we judge the question of consequential responsibility first and then work backwards to assign the relevant preventive responsibility. Pensions are probably the clearest example of this. Society generally requires people to make provision for their own retirement (preventive responsibility) because it regards the costs of old age as a matter of personal responsibility (in the consequential sense). In other words, it would not make sense for the government to expect people to assume responsibility for their old age if it was believed they had a right to assistance anyway.

A fourth kind of responsibility has to do with the conditions under which it is appropriate to make moral judgements of people's character or conduct. Let us call this *moral responsibility*. If morality has to do with the standards of right or good conduct to which individuals expect themselves and each other to conform, then someone is morally responsible for his or her actions when it is fitting to judge him or her by such standards, whether that judgement be praise or blame. Under what conditions is this fitting? Perhaps it wouldn't be right to morally judge someone for wrongdoing if he were in the grip of a mental illness which prevented him from acting otherwise. A more difficult case is if someone contravenes a moral standard because of a threat of harm by someone else. Suppose an employee is forced to steal money from his employers in order to secure the release of his child from some unscrupulous kidnappers. Although the kidnap does not absolve the employee from moral judgement – as it might do if he were temporarily insane – it is likely to change the content of the judgement. We don't blame him for what he did.

Once it has been established that someone is answerable from a moral perspective, the English language contains a vast number of different words to express moral approval or disapproval. We say a person is good, bad, considerate, thoughtless, decent, dishonourable, to name just a few. But notice that we also sometimes use the words 'responsible' and 'irresponsible' to express approval or disapproval. So we might say that someone is a responsible individual because he doesn't drop litter. Or we might say that such and such is an irresponsible person because he can't be relied upon in an emergency. In fact, we sometimes use 'responsible' and 'irresponsible' to pick out qualities of character or conduct associated with reflexive personal responsibility. I might say, for instance, that a friend acted responsibly by getting a job rather than living off the state. Or I might describe someone as acting irresponsibly when he racked up huge credit card debts which someone else was forced to pay off. The first person exhibits the virtue of self-reliance, while the second displays the vice of being a burden to others.

Why is it important to draw a distinction between consequential and moral responsibility? One reason is that there are occasions when it is appropriate to criticise someone for his or her actions but not to force him or her to bear the consequences. Take the following example due to the Harvard philosopher Thomas Scanlon:

> We can imagine a person who, as a result of generally horrible treatment as a child and lack of proper early training, is both undisciplined and unreliable. If this person lies to his employers, fails to do what he has agreed to do, and never exerts himself to get a job done, he is properly criticized for these actions and attitudes. But if they render him unemployable it would not be permissible to deny him welfare support on the ground that his unemployability is due to actions for which he is responsible. He is responsible (that is to say, open to criticism) for these actions, but he cannot simply be left to bear the consequences, since he has not had adequate opportunity to avoid being subject to them.[6]

Now some people might take the view that this person is neither morally responsible nor consequentially responsible for his actions. Others might hold that he is both morally and consequentially responsible. Even so, I do think that examples like this compel us to take seriously the possibility that someone could be morally blameworthy or full of vice without its being right to impose consequential responsibility.

On the other hand, it would be misleading to say – and I think Scanlon would agree about this – that people should be relieved of consequential responsibility *whenever* they have been subjected to a dysfunctional upbringing. It seems to matter what type of childhood is involved and what the context is. Consider a variation of the case due to Dworkin. Suppose the person concerned grew up within a poor council estate with high unemployment and was made to feel utterly worthless by his parents. In this case, holding him responsible for the consequences might not be the right thing to do. But compare his situation with that of an upper class toff who, despite being given every opportunity in life, drank away his inheritance and now cannot bring himself to work for a living because he was raised to think that such a life is beneath his class. It might be fair in the case of the toff both to condemn him for his attitude and to hold him responsible for its consequences.[7]

PERSONALLY RESPONSIBLE FOR WHAT?

Earlier in this chapter I characterised reflexive personal responsibility as the idea that individuals bear a special responsibility for the success or failure of their own lives. But what, more exactly, does success or failure mean?

One prominent idea is that individuals bear a special responsibility for their own well-being or welfare. The word 'welfare' has its origins in the idea of having a good trip or journey, but here it means how well a person's life goes. This is reflected in such phrases as 'social welfare', 'the welfare state' and 'welfare worker'. But whereas policymakers characteristically focus on the practical requirements of welfare such as employment, housing, social care and health, philosophers are more interested in developing a general conception of welfare. Three main conceptions are: hedonistic welfare (the psychological states that people experience when their lives go well, such as pleasure, happiness and enjoyment), success-based welfare (the successful achievement of preferences, ambitions, desires and deeper convictions about what gives value to life), and objective welfare (a list of things that make up an objectively good life, quite apart from what some misinformed or misguided individuals might think, such as loving relationships, meaningful work and play).[8]

It might seem obvious that people should be held personally responsible for their own welfare. Dworkin offers the case of Louis who reads magazines about the lifestyles of the rich and famous and deliberately sets out to cultivate expensive tastes even though he knows he will be unable to satisfy these tastes. Surely it can't be fair to expect the rest of society to subsidise his new tastes and give him the same happiness or preference satisfaction as everyone else.[9] But this might be a little premature. Even if it doesn't make sense for the state to assume primary responsibility for achieving equality of welfare, it could make sense for the state to provide equality of opportunity for welfare. As the American philosopher Richard Arneson puts it, 'The argument for equal opportunity rather than straight equality is simply that it is morally fitting to hold individuals responsible for the foreseeable consequences of their voluntary choices.'[10]

Of course, it might be insisted that the state can't be responsible for people's happiness, not even for opportunities for happiness, because the state simply isn't in a position to make people happy. Yet we already think of job satisfaction as an important determinate of people's welfare and something the state can measure and do something about. It is potentially only a short step from there to the claim that the state ought to take an interest in how satisfied people are with their lot, generally speaking. Indeed, David Cameron has recently argued that there is more to life than making money and, more importantly, that improving people's happiness is a key challenge for politicians.[11]

Another way of thinking about the objects of personal responsibility can be found in the work of Rawls. According to Rawls, the idea of personal responsibility is to be understood within a more general account of what it means to live in a well-ordered democratic society viewed as a system of fair cooperation among free and equal persons. The terms of fair cooperation also include a political conception of the appropriate roles for persons viewed as citizens and private individuals respectively. He writes:

citizens as a collective body, accepts responsibility for maintaining the equal basic liberties and fair equality of opportunity, and for providing a fair share of the primary goods for all within this framework; while citizens as individuals and associations accept responsibility for revising and adjusting their ends and aspirations in view of the all-purpose means they can expect, given their present and foreseeable situation.[12]

There is much in this division of responsibility to comment on. But for now I simply note that there are aspects of human well-being that cannot easily be classified either as primary goods (income and wealth) or as welfare (happiness and success). Medicine helps people avoid sickness and wheelchairs enable some people to get around more easily. But being healthy and being able to move around aren't resources. Nor are they forms of welfare. This point was first made by the Nobel Prize-winning economist Amartya Sen. He broke out of this terminological dilemma by introducing a new concept into the debate, that of *capability*. He argues that governments have a responsibility to protect and support the basic capabilities of all citizens, including the capability of being free from physical pain, being able to move around, being able to be well nourished and being able to live a long life.[13]

Nevertheless, Sen sometimes characterises the doings and beings (or *functionings*) that people actually achieve as a matter of personal responsibility. This means that it is down to society to provide people with basic capabilities, but down to individuals to turn their basic capabilities into achieved functionings. As the old saying goes, you can lead a horse to water, but you can't make it drink. I think this is right. But it is also worth pointing out that whether or not people enjoy basic capabilities at any given time can also depend to a greater or lesser degree on their previous choices. Thus suppose someone starts out in life with the capability of being free from pain, only to put this capability in jeopardy by engaging in adrenalin sports which carry a high risk of serious injury. These sorts of cases make it possible to ask whether or not people bear a special responsibility for their lifelong access to basic capabilities.

In this chapter I have offered a conceptual analysis of personal responsibility. Having introduced the core idea of reflexive personal responsibility I then outlined some different conceptions of what this means. I also distinguished between four different kinds of responsibility and described some of the things that individuals might be responsible for. In the next chapter I examine alternative accounts given by leading philosophers of the conditions under which it is appropriate to impose consequential responsibility.

3   What Do Philosophers Think? Part I

Brute luck is an enemy of just equality, and, since effects of genuine choice contrast with brute luck, genuine choice excuses otherwise unacceptable inequalities.

G. A. Cohen

The debate among philosophers concerning when it is, and when it is not, fair to impose consequential responsibility on individuals has become increasingly complex over the past 30 years or so. This chapter considers some of the main criteria. Most of the philosophers discussed here are liberal egalitarians, who affirm the values of liberty and equality. The state does not have the right, because of the importance of liberty, to abolish private property and the free market as Marxists prescribe. Nevertheless, the state should, contrary to the libertarian tradition, intervene to mitigate some of the more inegalitarian effects of the market. So liberal egalitarians do not think that all inequalities are unjust, but they are exercised by inequalities which reflect social hierarchy and circumstances of birth and upbringing. The trick is to figure out the exact point at which unjust inequalities end and personal responsibility begins.

CAUSES

A natural place to start thinking about consequential responsibility is with the idea that in order to be held responsible for his or her own disadvantages a person must be the cause of them. After all, people only discuss the possibility of asking smokers to pay more for their healthcare because they believe – quite correctly – that there is a causal link between smoking and an increased risk of developing certain diseases.

In the case of smoking, the causal link between the behaviour and the harm is well understood. Nevertheless, other judgements of causality can be fraught with difficulty. One common problem is how to select *the* operative cause among a number of possible causes. Reflect for a moment on the problem of unemployment. Suppose someone lives in an area where there is relatively high unemployment and not much demand for labour. This is one cause of unemployment. But now suppose he doesn't make much effort to attend his local Jobcentre and this apathy decreases his chances of finding work. This is a second cause. Nevertheless, suppose the local Jobcentre is poorly managed, has little useful information on job vacancies and poorly motivated staff. Here we have a third cause. Now imagine that this individual is the victim of racial stereotyping such that even if there were more opportunities available he would still find it difficult to secure a job. This is yet another cause. Bearing all this in mind, what is the *real* cause of his unemployment?

Even if a suitable way could be found to assign the real cause, however, it is still not obvious that being the cause of what happens to oneself should be a sufficient condition for being held consequentially responsible. Take an adult with severe learning difficulties and autism who keeps putting himself in harm's way because he lacks the concept of danger. If he runs the hot tap for too long and scalds his hands, there is a sense in which he was the cause of what happened to him. But it scarcely seems right to expect him to bear the consequences merely because he was the cause in the strict sense of the word. On the contrary, most people think that society has a responsibility to protect vulnerable people who are a danger to themselves. Of course, it is a further question as to *who* in society bears responsibility for such protection, whether it is family members, charities or government. In practice it may be that family members and charities do end up providing care for large numbers of vulnerable people, but it doesn't follow from this that they should be expected to do this alone or that it is fair for the government not to do its bit.

In my example, the individual lacked capacity. So let us now explore this idea as an alternative criterion for imposing consequential responsibility.

CAPACITY

That there can be no personal responsibility without capacity was an argument put forward by the philosopher H. L. A. Hart in relation to legal responsibility and punishment. 'What is crucial', according to Hart, 'is that those whom we punish should have had, when they acted, the normal capacities, physical and mental, for doing what the law requires and abstaining from what it forbids, and a fair opportunity to exercise these capacities'. Capacity in this sense has both a cognitive and a volitional aspect. The cognitive aspect says that a person must have the capacity to understand the circumstances in which he finds himself and to be able to reason about the nature and likely consequences of his actions. The volitional aspect says that a person must have the capacity to be able to control his conduct in the sense of having an ability to act or not act in certain ways. Part of the attraction of this view is that it captures the intuition that it is wrong to punish someone who 'could not have helped it' but right to punish someone who could have done otherwise but 'just didn't stop and think'.[1]

It may be tempting to appeal to something like Hart's capacity test when thinking about access to social welfare. Consider the alternatives. Suppose we make the relevant test whether or not welfare claimants intentionally make themselves worse off in order to get assistance. One reason for concentrating on capacity rather than on what people intend to do is the practical point that it is notoriously difficult to know a person's state of mind after the event. Do we want to live in a world where the welfare state employs psychologists to determine whether or not a person deliberately set out to become homeless before we can say whether or not he ought to receive public housing? More importantly, a great many people simply fail to think about the consequences of their actions. They don't intentionally set out to become destitute so that others will feel compelled to help them. Rather, they don't appreciate the consequences of what they are doing because they don't bother to stop and think. I dare say that someone who acts intentionally or recklessly in worsening his personal circumstances has a weaker case for public assistance than someone who embarked upon a course of action thoughtlessly. But it does seem plausible that a theory of consequential responsibility should be able to recognise negligence as grounds for holding people personally responsible.

Rawls, for one, puts capacity at the centre of his account of personal responsibility, although capacity is conceived differently than in the case of Hart. Rawls maintains that in a well-ordered democratic society it is appropriate to regard citizens as having 'two moral powers': the capacity for a sense of justice and the capacity for a conception of the good. Together these powers give people the ability to adjust their likes and dislikes over the course of their lives to the income and wealth they can reasonably expect to receive within a just society. What level of income and wealth people can reasonably expect to receive depends, in part, on the level that would be required to safeguard the long-term development and exercise of their two moral powers. Rawls' argument is that having the two moral powers is part of the way in which members of well-ordered democratic societies regard each other and not unreasonably so. In that sense the nature and significance of these powers is 'political not metaphysical'.[2]

CONTROL

Other philosophers, by contrast, believe that capacity is merely a surface condition and that what really matters is whether or not people exercise control in a metaphysical sense. According to G. A. Cohen, an egalitarian political philosopher and scholar of Karl Marx, society should compensate disadvantages which are due to factors that lie beyond a person's voluntary control, but not factors that do lie within a person's control.[3] On this view, having the *capacity* to decide how to live is a secondary phenomenon: it is *control* that counts. This becomes clear when the two come apart. A person may have the capacity to decide how to live in the sense that he is able to revise his likes and dislikes over time and make choices about how to live. Yet, as Arneson points out, it is likely that people have different choice making and choice-following capacities which may in turn depend on a complex combination of genetic inheritance and social circumstances over which they exercise little or no control.[4]

It is an implication of this view that a decision lies within a person's voluntary control only if he or she exercises free will. According to one definition, someone exercises free will only if he or she could have decided to act differently than he or she actually did with everything else remaining the same. For this to be the case there cannot have existed for that person a set of antecedent conditions that made acting in a particular way inescapable. This has important implications for how we think about consequential responsibility. Cohen maintains that even if someone decides to develop a taste for expensive things, we must leave space for the possibility that he lacks ultimate control over the personality traits, family upbringing, life experiences, and so on, which together caused him to decide to develop that expensive taste. So if the philosophical theory of hard determinism is true, then *prima facie* no individual should be held responsible for unequal happiness or preference satisfaction which results from such tastes.[5]

This is, however, certainly not the position of other contemporary philosophers. Hart, for example, argues that it is hard to avoid the conclusion that people should be held liable for their criminal acts regardless of the thesis of hard determinism.[6] Dworkin likewise insists that people commonly accept responsibility for the success or failure of their own lives without assuming they have full control over the contents of their choices and personalities.[7] Indeed, according to Dworkin:

> We might think ourselves persuaded, intellectually, of the philosophical thesis that people have no free will, and that we are no more causally responsible for our fate when it is the upshot of our choices than when it flows only from a handicap or from society's distribution of wealth. But we cannot lead a life out of that philosophical conviction. We cannot plan or judge our lives except by distinguishing what we must take responsibility for, because we chose it, and what we cannot take responsibility for because it was beyond our control.[8]

I find this convincing. But I also think there are other aspects to personal responsibility which are much more than planning our lives. Taking personal responsibility can be a way of affirming our personal identity. Arguably we understand who we are as individuals, in part, through the personal responsibilities we assume during the course of our lives. That I assume personal responsibility for my children, for the cleanliness of my workspace and for my own trials and tribulations is the kind of person I take myself to be. In this way personal responsibility is intimately bound up with my conception of self.

I suspect that assuming personal responsibility is also about affirming ownership. That is, we accept personal responsibility partly because this is a way of staking a claim on our lives. I think that I am responsible for my life, rather than other people, because I believe that it is *my* life rather than anyone else's. It seems to me that there are good reasons for doing these things even if hard determinism is true.

CHOICE VERSUS BRUTE LUCK

Dworkin's preferred distinction is between 'choice' and 'brute luck'. On this view, 'individuals should be relieved of consequential responsibility for those unfortunate features of their situation that are brute luck, but not from those that should be seen as flowing from their own choices'.[9] The distinction between choice and brute luck can be understood in different ways, but one example that should help to fix ideas for the present purposes involves two persons, both suffering from liver failure. The first person's situation does not reflect choices that she has made or is making or would make, because her liver failure resulted from a cancer to which she was genetically predisposed. The second person's liver failure, by contrast, does reflect choices he has made, since it was caused by his excessive drinking. So we might say that the first person should be relieved of some or all of the costs of her treatment, but the second person should not.

Dworkin draws a further distinction between 'brute luck' and 'option luck'. 'Option luck is a matter of how deliberate and calculated gambles turn out – whether someone gains or loses through accepting an isolated risk he or she should have anticipated and might have declined. Brute luck is a matter of how risks fall out that are not in that sense deliberate gambles.'[10] So, for example, if someone chooses to spend his money on lottery scratch cards and doesn't win, then the bad luck is his and nobody else's. He has no claim in fairness to his money back. Even so, the idea of a 'deliberate and calculated' gamble requires at least some level of knowledge of the possible outcomes, which includes not only an awareness of the outcomes but also some understanding of what they mean and how likely they are. It would be unfair to regard something as option luck if through no fault of his own the alleged gambler had no clue of the dangers he was facing or was blamelessly mistaken about the chances of those being the consequences.

The distinction between choice and brute luck is one attempt to specify which inequalities are fair, and therefore should be borne by the individuals themselves, and which are unfair, and therefore should be addressed by the state acting on behalf of society as a whole. One reason for making the cut in this way, aside from any intuitive appeal it might have, is that it enables or purports to enable the state to remain neutral between different conceptions of the good life. Other things remaining equal, it is wrong for the state to judge one kind of life as intrinsically superior to any other kind of life. Holding persons responsible for 'good' or 'bad' lives would inevitably lead the state to make such judgements. But to hold persons responsible for the consequences of their choices but not for the consequences of their brute luck does not comment on whether a life is good or bad and is in that sense neutral.

This criterion is not without its problems, however. It says that people should be held responsible for the consequences of their choices. But it isn't always so obvious what those consequences are. Suppose Bob likes to play rugby and although he is advised to wear protective headgear he chooses not to. During a match he suffers a head injury. Were it not for his choice, he would not have suffered the injury. So this consequence is one he ought to bear. But while recovering at home from his head injury, Bob accidentally stumbles over a table leg, falls to the floor and seriously damages his back. We now have to make a judgement about whether this secondary consequence (the fact that he has injured his back) is part of the relevant consequences of his initial choice. Suppose further that while recovering from the back injury Bob catches pneumonia. Here we have a third possible consequence of his choice. On the one hand, if he hadn't chosen not to wear the headgear, he wouldn't have banged his head, tripped over the table leg or caught pneumonia. On the other hand, intuitively there seems to be a difference between the immediate consequence and what happens after that.

A similar problem applies to luck. Suppose a tiny meteorite falls from the sky, striking you on the foot. Some months later, after a very long, painful recovery, you think to yourself, 'Boy, I was lucky the meteorite didn't land on my head.' Then you check yourself, 'How was I lucky? If I were lucky, it wouldn't have hit me at all!' In fact, 'If I were really lucky, it would have fallen in my garden and be worth £1 million.' The point of the story is that luck is either good or bad only relative to some baseline. So the question is: which baseline? Is the relevant baseline the best thing that could have happened to you in all possible worlds or the worst thing that could have happened? Or maybe the relevant comparison is with what happens to other people in the real world. But which other people? Perhaps you are luckier than someone who was struck by lightning. Then again, you are not as lucky as someone who won the lottery. In the absence of sensible answers to these questions, the vague idea that we should try to mitigate brute luck is useless because it doesn't tell us what to mitigate.[11]

These problems speak to the usefulness of the choice/brute luck distinction. Other philosophers, by contrast, question the moral standing of its consequences. The American philosopher Elizabeth Anderson dubs this theory 'luck egalitarianism' and she argues that luck egalitarians have fundamentally misunderstood the point of equality. Why so? Because to focus on the distinction between voluntary choice and brute luck implies that those people who take deliberate gambles should be left to suffer the consequences no matter how bad, while those who experience bad luck are owed contemptuous pity rather than genuine egalitarian concern.[12] Similarly, Samuel Scheffler writes:

Most people do not insist, as a general matter, that someone who makes a bad decision thereby forfeits all claims to assistance. They do not take such a sweeping view either in matters of personal morality or in political contexts. In their personal lives, for example, they do not refuse to comfort a friend whose foolish, but voluntarily undertaken, romance has come to a painful end; or to give directions to a driver who has predictably become lost after failing to consult a map; or to help a family member who finds himself unemployed as a result of a poor career choice. In short, most people do not have a blanket policy of refusing assistance to anyone who has made a mistake or a poor decision. Such a policy would strike us as harsh, unforgiving, insensitive to context, and unduly moralistic.[13]

These sorts of arguments can have a lot of rhetorical force, but for reasons of balance it is important to keep in mind that most of the writers labelled 'luck egalitarians' do not actually claim that *every* instance of voluntary choice should incur full responsibility or that every instance of brute luck merits contemptuous pity or even full compensation. This is for two reasons. First, they believe that holding persons responsible for the consequences of their choices depends on background conditions of equality of opportunity and since these conditions are not satisfied in the cases discussed by Anderson and Scheffler, they cannot claim that luck egalitarians would abandon these people. Second, they believe that where the conditions for offering compensation are satisfied, the aim of compensation is to show equal respect for people not to pity them. Moreover, they insist paying compensation is something authorities should do, all things considered, so that levels of compensation shouldn't bankrupt society as a whole.[14]

SECOND-ORDER ATTITUDES

Many philosophers take the view that society does not owe compensation to people with expensive tastes. Some take this view because they assume most people possess the capacity to revise their tastes. Others instead highlight the fact that people normally identify with their tastes, which is a kind of second-order attitude.

This line of thought can be traced back to Harry Frankfurt's case of the willing drug addict. This addict is unusual in that he fully identifies with the life he leads in the sense that he doesn't regret the cravings that compel him to go out and commit robberies. This, according to Frankfurt, may be sufficient to justify holding the addict morally responsible for his actions even though they are in a sense involuntary.[15]

Dworkin extends the same reasoning to the question of expensive tastes. He argues that the state should not subsidise people who prefer the finer things in life not merely because doing so would be massively expensive but because doing so would be inconsistent with our ordinary ethical distinctions and practices. Since people ordinarily identify with their personal tastes, in the sense that they don't regret having them but instead regard them as defining their goals in life, it would be 'bizarre' to offer them compensation for their tastes. It would be to ignore the fact that we have the tastes we do because of our judgements about what makes life worth living.[16]

According to Cohen, however, Dworkin has missed the point about expensive tastes. While it may or may not be bizarre for someone to regret his own tastes and preferences, it certainly wouldn't be strange for someone to regret the fact that he lives in a world where a certain price is attached to the things he likes beyond his control. Cohen offers the example of Paul, who loves photography, and Fred, who loves fishing. Paul's problem is that he cannot afford to pursue his love of photography, because it just so happens that in his particular society photography is very expensive. The upshot is that he has less enjoyment than Fred, who loves fishing, a much cheaper pastime in that society. According to Cohen, Paul suffers bad luck due to the high price of photography and therefore has a redistributive claim against the rest of his society for subsidies.[17]

But the disagreement doesn't end there. Dworkin insists that although we might think of Paul as suffering from bad 'price luck', this doesn't warrant redistributive claims against others. Price luck is not the same as brute luck. The price is itself the result of other people's tastes and preferences and we tend to think of this network of tastes and preferences as forming the background conditions of justice, not as forms of compensable brute luck. If, on the other hand, Paul is actually the victim of some form of craving or obsession for photography which he cannot control, then it might be fair to provide him with assistance on the grounds of bad 'preference luck'. But in that case the assistance is offered in respect of the psychological handicap not in respect of his lack of preference satisfaction. We can distinguish the two thoughts by saying that Paul has a claim for subsidised therapy rather than for subsidised photography.[18]

EQUALITY OF OPPORTUNITY

Another supposed condition for imposing consequential responsibility on individuals that I have already hinted at a couple of times is the fact that choices will only justify otherwise unacceptable disadvantages if they are made against a background of equality of opportunity. The basic thought is that it cannot be fair to hold someone responsible for his choice of A rather than B if he did not have the same or a comparable set of options to choose between as other people; that is, if he did not have the opportunity to choose between A, B, C, D, E and others did have this opportunity.[19]

It is worth pausing for a moment to reflect on just how demanding this sort of condition for responsibility could be given the enormous inequalities of background opportunities that characterise Britain and many other societies. In a society where a significant proportion of the population are born into conditions of poverty and lack of opportunity, while others find it relatively easy to achieve comfortable and fulfilling lives with minimal effort, it is much harder to make a case for imposing consequential responsibility on the former. Of course, we may still think it appropriate to morally criticise people for not trying.

While there is support among liberal egalitarian philosophers for something like the equality of opportunity condition, applying the idea to actual societies can be difficult. One difficulty stems from the fact that the opportunities someone has at any given moment of her life will naturally depend on her prior choices. Failing to seize an opportunity now has a tendency to limit opportunities later. For this reason, most philosophers working in this field regard the ideal of equality of opportunity as applying to an entire life rather than at given moments. Arneson, for example, argues that equality of opportunity for welfare is achieved when at the outset of adult life – at the age of 18, for example – every person has the same expected welfare as everybody else provided everyone makes reasonable choices.[20] The obvious practical difficulty here is how to determine with a reasonable degree of certainty whether or not at the outset of life someone has the same expected welfare as other people. How could we ever be sure of that?

A second difficulty is that even if someone did not enjoy equality of opportunity at the start of his adult life, this does not always make it appropriate to set aside personal responsibility for the choices he makes. Consider the case of someone whose circumstances are such that the only jobs available to him at the age of 18 all involve low-paid, tedious manual labour. (Many other 18-year-olds in his society enjoy a much wider spectrum of jobs from which they can choose including high-paid, creative complex labour.) Suppose he decides to forgo the available jobs. Do we really wish to say that he may be absolved of full responsibility merely because he did not have the opportunity to work as a doctor or lawyer? Doesn't he have a responsibility to try to make the best of a bad situation?

A third difficulty concerns the definition of equality of opportunity. Some examples seem more clear-cut than others. I think few people would deny that a person who had to beg and grovel for work due to the racist attitudes of local employers has unequal opportunities as compared to someone who merely had to fill out a form and shake hands with the boss. Likewise, someone who needs an expensive wheelchair and access facilities does not, other things remaining equal, enjoy the same opportunities for employment as someone who can easily catch the bus. However, what should we say about someone who is not permitted to accept the only jobs currently available to him because these jobs involve tasks which conflict with his religious beliefs? Does he have lesser opportunity than someone who is not limited by these same beliefs? Some philosophers insist that someone in this position *does* have the opportunity to accept these jobs; it is simply that he chooses not to make use of that opportunity. Others, by contrast, argue that taking a job is not a real opportunity for an agent if it does not form part of his or her permissible range of actions, such as when the job is ruled out by his or her religious commitments.[21]

DESERVINGNESS

Yet another pertinent criterion for deciding questions of consequential responsibility has to do with the commonly held intuition that individuals ought to get what they deserve. A theory of just deserts is one way of answering questions of consequential responsibility because giving people what they deserve can be a way of holding them responsible for their situations. In fact, two of the most prominent philosophers currently working on these issues have at times slipped into the language of deservingness when expressing the idea of consequential responsibility.[22]

Appealing to the criterion of just deserts underscores the importance of dividing personal responsibility into its positive and negative forms. To say that someone should be held personally responsible for a positive outcome is to say that he or she should reap the benefits of that outcome. Hence, we can ask whether or not the most talented and hard-working people in our society deserve more income than the least talented and hard-working people. Conversely, to say that someone should be held personally responsible for a negative outcome is to say that he or she may be left to bear the burden. Charles Murray, for example, distinguishes between 'the case of the man who has worked steadily for many years and, in his fifties, is thrown out of his job because the factory closes', and the man who is 'healthy and in the prime of life', but 'refuses to work'. Murray claims that an ethically sensitive social policy would discriminate between such people according to their deserts.[23]

Of course, once we allow just deserts into the picture we are likely to get different results than if we simply focus on assessments of voluntary choice. Consider the example of Mother Teresa, who unselfishly devoted her life to helping the sick and the starving on the streets of Calcutta. What is interesting about Mother Teresa in the context of the present discussion is that because she acted with virtue we tend to ignore the fact that she acted imprudently in the sense that she deliberately risked her own health and safety to help others. Perhaps there are many reasons why society should support this kind of action. We might suppose that the people helped by good deeds have been the victims of past injustices. In this way people like Mother Teresa become instruments of social justice as well as instruments of God. But let us concentrate on the choice itself. Placing all the emphasis on personal choice might imply that individuals who choose to devote their lives to doing good deeds for others ought to be held responsible for the consequences of their choices. This might imply, for instance, that carers or people involved in community work have no excuse for not looking for paid employment when it comes to receiving out of work benefits from the state. Yet, as Arneson argues, in such cases it seems more fitting all things considered to waive the responsibility otherwise implied by voluntary choice in order to recognise 'virtuous imprudence'.[24] Similar judgements might apply in the case of someone who breaks his leg while rescuing a child from the path of a speeding truck.[25]

REASONABLENESS

Another important criterion is reasonabless. In some instances the word 'reasonable' is used with a narrow scope, as when we claim, 'X's bad situation resulted from what was otherwise reasonable behaviour on his part, so it wouldn't be fair to hold him responsible for his situation.' In this case, we attribute the quality of reasonableness to the behaviour and use this as a basis for waiving responsibility. As one might expect, there are different ways of determining whether or not someone's behaviour is or was reasonable. One method is to examine how similar types of people behave in comparable situations. A variant of this looks at people's role responsibilities. So, for example, we might judge that it is fitting not to hold firefighters, police officers and members of the armed forces responsible for the risk of injury and death associated with their particular roles. What is reasonable conduct for a firefighter, in other words, might be unreasonable for ordinary citizens. That being said, even firefighters must behave reasonably in carrying out their tasks, where this implies following the techniques and safety guidelines learned during training. (Acts of heroism are another matter and fall under the previous criterion.) An alternative way of judging narrow reasonableness is in terms of unreasonable burdens. Consider Sen's case of Mr Kedra Mia, a Muslim daily labourer who every day would travel to work in a Hindu neighbourhood despite the threat to his life. In the end Mr Kedra Mia was stabbed and killed. But suppose he had refused to take the risk. Arguably in this event his lack of employment would not have been his own responsibility since he would have acted reasonably by refusing to put his life in danger.[26]

In other instances, by contrast, the word 'reasonable' is used with a wide scope, as when we claim, 'It wouldn't be reasonable to hold X responsible for his bad situation, even though it was the result of his voluntary choice, because imposing responsibility on him now will ruin his life for ever.' Or when we claim, 'It just isn't reasonable to make someone bear the consequences when his mistakes were only small and the consequences so massive.' Here we say nothing – at least, nothing explicitly – about the reasonableness or otherwise of the behaviour. Instead we refer to the reasonableness of imposing personal responsibility. Once again, there are different ways of judging reasonableness. Roughly, the Aristotelian tradition will underscore the importance of proportionality, so that the consequences are in some sense proportional to the actions. The utilitarian tradition will balance the expected utility of the individual who is held or not held responsible against the expected utility of the larger society in the event that responsibility is imposed or waived. The aim will be to impose or waive personal responsibility in such a way as to maximise net utility. The contractualist tradition, by contrast, will emphasise the requirement of reasonable agreement.[27] To give one illustration, Anderson maintains that any proposed allocation of consequential responsibility should satisfy what she calls 'the test of interpersonal justification'. According to this test, 'any consideration offered as a reason for a policy must serve to justify that policy when uttered by anyone else who participates in the economy as a worker or consumer.' Drawing on a feminist tradition in political theory, Anderson offers the following example, 'The principle "let us assign others to discharge our caretaking obligations to dependants, and attach such meagre benefits to performance of this role that these caretakers live at our mercy" cannot survive the test of interpersonal justification.'[28]

Obviously the practical difference between narrow and wide scope reasonableness will be more or less significant depending on how they are defined. It may be that wide scope reasonableness incorporates narrow reasonableness and vice versa.

RECIPROCITY

So far I have introduced various criteria for determining whether or not it is fair for the state to hold persons responsible for the situations in which they find themselves. This is *fairness as appropriately holding persons responsible*. Another way of framing questions of personal responsibility and fairness starts from a slightly different perspective: everyone who wishes to enjoy a share of the benefits of social cooperation owes a corresponding respon-sibility to contribute something to that society in return. This is *fairness as reciprocity*.

Arguments from fairness as reciprocity are sometimes couched in the language of people's role responsibilities, specifically, the role responsibilities of citizens. Stuart White develops this sort of view in his 2003 book *The Civic Minimum: On the Rights and Obligations of Economic Citizenship*. He stresses that his pre-ferred conception of reciprocity does not demand that citizens' contributions be strictly proportional or equivalent in value to the benefits they receive. It is enough, he argues, for citizens to provide an appropriate good or service in return, one that meets the weaker test of being a decent contribution and suited to their abilities and circumstances. There are many possible ways of fleshing out this idea, but White focuses on the idea of a basic work expectation, or 'civic labour'. One example might be lone parents in receipt of welfare benefits who make the contribution of bringing up the next generation of citizens.[29]

The idea of fairness as reciprocity is also used by philosophers in the field of healthcare. It is suggested that applying the distinc-tion between choice and brute luck would be too harsh in respect of forms of ill-health resulting from choices and too generous in respect of forms of ill-health resulting from brute luck, potentially justifying a 'bottomless pit' of public expenditure. What we need instead is a type of solidaristic reciprocity in healthcare. What is required is not necessarily forcing persons to make the right contributions to the healthcare system as a condition of receiving healthcare, although this may be justified in some cases. Rather, the important thing is to encourage persons to act responsibly, such as by trying to adopt a healthy lifestyle, following doctor's orders and not making excessive demands on healthcare serv-ices.[30]

Although reciprocity-based arguments often focus on role responsibilities, the question remains what happens when indi-vidual members of society fail to do their bit. Getting clear on what the reciprocal contributions should be can shed light on why it is right to hold persons responsible in the consequential sense. So if the state, acting on behalf of society, requires persons to contribute to the economy in some way or to act responsibly in relation to their own health as a matter of patient responsibilities, then the fact that certain persons refuse to contribute or act in these ways might furnish the state with a justification for withdrawing benefits or healthcare. Be that as it may, we are still left with the thorny task of working out what people's contributions should be in the first place. And the answer to *that* question cannot be 'Persons ought to contribute in ways for which it is fair to hold them consequentially responsible.' Otherwise the whole argument becomes circular.

EQUAL SHARES

All of the criteria discussed so far have to do with fairness in one form or another. But these criteria are only one part of the story. Many contemporary philosophers believe that it is right to pursue fairness, but they also disagree about what fairness is. Some philosophers affirm that holding persons responsible in appropriate ways is the right kind of fairness. Others concentrate on the idea of expecting citizens to do their bit. In both instances personal responsibility is put to the forefront. But other philosophers interpret fairness differently such that there is much less room for personal responsibility. In other words, forms of responsibility-sensitivity that might be appropriate under some conceptions of fairness might not be appropriate when fairness is understood differently.

To be more specific, some philosophers support the idea of an unconditional basic income as a way of treating all citizens fairly. Unconditional basic income is a flat-rate, non-means-tested income paid to every citizen, whether or not they are working and independently of the above criteria. There are a number of arguments supporting unconditional basic income and we shall come across some of them in later chapters. But one argument starts with the fundamental assumption that everyone has a right to an equal share of the earth's natural resources, even those who aren't in paid employment, with shares to be paid by other members of society. We might call this *fairness as equal shares*. Unconditional basic income is sometimes presented as a 'rent' to be paid by those who currently possess or benefit from an unequally large share of the earth's natural resources.[31]

This argument for unconditional basic income cannot be taken as read, however. For one thing, there remain difficult questions concerning the level of basic income. If the level is set too high, then it may be a tremendous burden on taxpayers. It might also discourage people from entering the labour market. If the level is set too low, then the income might be enough for beach bums but not enough for other, more vulnerable groups, such as lone parents and the disabled who have special expenses. In addition to this, it is worth making the point that expecting all taxpayers to pay for the share of resources given to every newborn child potentially ignores the responsibility of parents for bringing these additional persons into the world. The American philosopher Eric Rakowski writes:

> If new people just appeared in the world from time to time, like fresh boatloads of unwitting settlers, and did not owe their birth to the actions of present members of society, then the foregoing principles would in fact come into play. But babies are not brought by storks whose whims are beyond our control. Specific individuals are responsible for their existence. It is therefore unjust to declare, as the above principles do, that because two people decide to have a child, or through carelessness find themselves with one, *everyone* is required to share their resources with the new arrival, and to the same extent as its parents. With what right can two people force all the rest, through deliberate behavior rather than bad brute luck, to settle for less than their fair shares after resources have been divided

justly? If the cultivation of expensive tastes, or silly gambles, or any other intentional action cannot give rise to redistributive claims, how can procreation?'[32]

COMBINING CRITERIA

Let us take stock. We have seen that the philosophical litera-ture throws up a bewildering array of criteria for determining when and how far it is fair to hold persons responsible for their disadvantages and when, in contrast to this, society at large ought to provide assistance. How do we turn these criteria into a consistent set of policies?

There are a number of problems to overcome. The first is epis-temological. Some philosophers identify control as a core condi-tion for holding or not holding persons responsible. The problem being that it is notoriously difficult to have veridical knowledge of what does and does not lie within a person's control. Yet Cohen remains unapologetic. As he ironically puts it, 'we may indeed be up to our necks in the free will problem, but that is just tough luck. It is not a reason for not following the argument where it goes.'[33] This may or may not be sound advice as far as 'the truth' is concerned. But if political philosophers are concerned about the interface between their discipline and public policy, they should think twice before going down this particular road. My point is not simply that policymakers are ill-equipped to resolve the free will problem. Even if a respectable theory of free will could be sought, policymakers would still have to find a way to apply that theory. Thus suppose for the sake of argument that having free will consists in an ultimate ability to choose otherwise. How could public officials discover whether or not a person had the ability to choose differently than he or she actually did choose?

Other conditions for imposing responsibility do not fare much better on this score. Imagine if public authorities tried to be more sensitive to the distinction between personal choice (which includes people's preferences and ambitions) and circumstances (which includes not only family upbringing but also natural talent and other genetic endowments). The problem is that it seems pretty obvious that people's fates are determined by a combination of choices *and* circumstances. Talents develop over time and the decision to develop talent is based on a person's ambition. Moreover, just how much ambition people possess depends on how much raw talent they have to work with initially. Family life can also play a part in determining levels of ambition. So, how do officials identify at any particular time that component of personal disadvantage that is traceable to differential circumstances as distinguished from differential ambition?

Dworkin dubs this 'the strategic problem' and his answer is rather ingenious. He invites the reader to think about what level and type of insurance people would purchase if they had the same antecedent chance of suffering various misfortunes (including low talent, ill-health and being born to poor parents) and the same opportunity to purchase insurance. Even if welfare planners cannot separate out that proportion of disadvantage which is due to choice and circumstances respectively, they can try to bring people closer to the level of resources they would have achieved had they purchased insurance under hypothetical conditions of equality.[34] Nevertheless this hypothetical insurance strategy raises its own epistemological problems. How could the welfare official know for sure what people would have purchased if contrary to fact they had the same chance of misfortune? How could anyone know for sure? No doubt welfare officials could take some clues from the insurance industry concerning the sorts of policies people purchase and how much they are willing to pay for them. But the rest is open to speculation.

Sometimes policy strategists at the heart of government make an appeal to philosophical criteria, seemingly oblivious to the epistemological problems I have outlined. In February 2004, for example, the Prime Minister's Strategy Unit published a discussion paper which identified the choice/luck distinction as an appropriate tool for dividing responsibility. It states: 'This has been characterised as a presumption that individuals should take responsibility for their "knowingly taken life-choices" (for good or bad) while the state or community should seek to attenuate "brute luck" effects, such as result from family social background.'[35] Yet there is little awareness in this discussion paper of the pitfalls associated with applying this distinction in the real world. There is no mention of the problem that people's life-choices are intimately bound up with their social and familial backgrounds. Public authorities may never have the information they need to separate out the affects of personal choice and brute luck.

A further complication yet to be addressed is the fact that many of the aforementioned criteria are a matter of degree. For instance, it would be odd to say that there is an absolute distinction between being deserving and not being deserving. The element of choice can also be represented as a matter of degree, not least because genuine choice depends on information and people can have more or less information at different times and for different reasons.[36] Consequently, we might be tempted to offer the following rule of thumb: the more the relevant criteria are satisfied, the less people can object to being held personally responsible. On the other hand, perhaps we want to say that there is at least a minimum amount that each criterion must be satisfied before personal responsibility becomes appropriate. But then we are faced with the difficult task of specifying the minimum degree of capacity, choice, opportunity, desert and reasonableness that is required in order for someone to attract personal responsibility.

Notwithstanding these complications, suppose these criteria can be specified in some tolerably adequate way. Which, if any, of the above criteria are necessary grounds for imposing personal responsibility? Which, if any, are sufficient grounds?

It seems to me that having capacity is a necessary condition for imposing personal responsibility but not a sufficient condition. Surely it wouldn't be fair to hold someone consequentially responsible for failing to avoid danger if he lacked the physical or mental wherewithal to do so. Indeed, in order to judge whether or not people are deserving of assistance or whether or not they acted reasonably or whether or not they have made an acceptable contribution to society we first need to know something about their capacity. On the other hand, simply because someone has an appropriate set of capacities, that doesn't mean he or she ought to bear the consequences of everything he or she does or doesn't do. Sometimes people exercise their mental and physical capacities in taking risks, the consequences of which are rightly shared among society as a whole. Take the firefighter who runs into a burning building to save a child and ends up with third-degree burns and large medical bills, for example.

Control in the metaphysical sense of the word is perhaps neither necessary nor sufficient. As we have seen, some philosophers believe that we are up to our necks in the free will problem. Be that as it may, if philosophers are to reflect people's ordinary intuitions, then perhaps we should say that individuals ought to bear the consequences of their choices even if there is no free will.

Equality of opportunity, at first glance, seems to be a necessary condition for imposing consequential responsibility. On closer inspection, however, it is not clear that starting out in life without the benefit of strict equality of opportunity can excuse someone who makes no effort to make the best of a bad situation. That said, a person who starts out with virtually no opportunities at all has a much stronger claim for exculpation than someone who starts out with more than his fair share of opportunities.

A number of other criteria, namely deservingness, reasonableness and contribution to society, also appear to be relevant but not decisive in their own right. That someone gives something back to society may be grounds for waiving a degree of responsibility for income (say). But from the mere fact that a surfer makes a contribution by picking up litter from the beach for an hour each day, it doesn't automatically follow that all personal responsibility is wiped from the slate such that he can fairly be expected to earn the same as an accountant.

Similarly, the idea that every individual is entitled to a[n] share of the earth's natural resources only takes us so far: for th[ere] is a sense in which forcing other taxpayers, many of whom ma[y] choose to have one child or no children at all, to pay for the share of resources owed to all newcomers to the community is itself an abdication of personal responsibility on the part of adults who decide to have more children than they can afford to provide for.

Given this picture of multiple criteria, we must now turn our minds to scenarios in which one or more criteria support imposing personal responsibility, while one or more criteria favour waiving personal responsibility. Of course, things would be straightforward if, no matter what set of criteria are used, the same people should always be held responsible. But there is no clear evidence for this. There might be some convergence in the incidence of the different criteria, but we cannot count on that being true across the board. On the contrary, we might find that persons ought to be held responsible according to the criterion of choice but not according to other criteria such as desert or reasonableness.

Philosophers will divide at this point. Some may hold out the hope of establishing a rigid hierarchy between the criteria, meaning that if one criterion is superior to a second, then it should always take precedence whenever there is disparity. Others, by contrast, might say that it is not possible to establish such an order of priority among these criteria. What we have are a number of *pro tanto* criteria, that is to say, criteria which only have so much weight against each other. It is simply vague, for example, how much weight should be given to the fact that somebody is very badly off as a result of consciously choosing to give up her career to become a stay at home mother; that she formed her preferences against the backdrop of societal gender norms; that she nevertheless identifies with her preferences; that it may or may not be in the interests of society to subsidise stay at home mothers who could go out to work; that as well as being a stay at home mother she also works part-time as an unpaid fund raiser for a children's hospital; that some women in her situation

work, while others do not; and so on. The
t so much that it is impossible to develop a
e relative weight of the different criteria but
dexes could seem equally fair and there is no
een them at the level of first principle. That is,
tforwardly claim to be *the fairest*.

Even if the second group of philosophers are right, however,
we might still try to formulate rough generalisations which could
provide a guide when criteria conflict. Consider what we might
call *the rule of aggregation*: if public officials are faced with a
decision between holding someone personally responsible for
a situation and not holding the person responsible, and each
option is supported by one or more conflicting criteria, then they
should choose whichever option commands the greatest number
of criteria. The obvious problem with the rule of aggregation,
however, is that it overlooks the very real possibility that some
criteria could carry more weight than others. So even if a higher
number of criteria point in favour of holding someone personally
responsible than not holding the person responsible, this doesn't
necessarily mean that this should carry the day. A single criterion
could outweigh two or more criteria. The task of aggregation is
further complicated by the fact that any given criterion may carry
more or less weight in different contexts and when compared
with different criteria and when considered by different people
according to their own intuitions.

What conclusions can we draw from all of this? One is that
whether one is committed to rigid hierarchies or more flexible,
intuitionistic judgements of personal responsibility it would be
helpful to know a little bit more about what ordinary people
think about these different criteria. I shall explore public opinion
in Chapter 6. A second is that public officials need more guidance on implementing the relevant criteria than philosophers
have given so far. Not only do they need more guidance on how
to overcome the epistemological problems mentioned above
but also more guidance on how to weigh the different criteria.

Perhaps philosophers are simply unable to give this guidance because there is no way to solve the epistemological problems and no one correct index for the criteria. In which case, we need some other method. So I shall try to develop a democratic answer in Chapter 8.

4 What Do Philosophers Think? Part II

We ought to look on it as a mark of goodness in God that he has put us in this life under a necessity of labour: not only to keep mankind from the mischiefs that ill men at leisure are very apt to do; but it is a benefit even to the good or the virtuous, which are thereby preserved from the ills of idleness or the diseases that attend constant study in a sedentary life.

John Locke

Intuitively personal responsibility seems to have as much to do with the notion of living well as with fair shares. Besides, you might ask, who really wants to live in a society where all the government does is insist on fairness to every last penny? Shouldn't government also promote the good life? With this thought in mind, let us now travel beyond the narrow confines of the previous chapter and consider why else we care about personal responsibility. It seems to me that any plausible answer to the question 'Why does personal responsibility matter?' should also provide a ready answer to the question 'When does personal responsibility matter?' If the answer to the first question is 'Because it makes people economically better off', for example, then it is possible that the answer to the second question is 'Most of the time, but not in times of recession'. If, on the other hand, the answer to the first question is 'Because it is part of the good life', then it is quite possible that the answer to the second question is 'Almost all of the time'.

UTILITY

The claim that personal responsibility is a moral good can take many forms. Let us start with the proposition that personal responsibility matters instrumentally, to the extent that it has beneficial consequences for both individuals and society as a whole. This immediately raises two questions. First, what beneficial consequences do we care about? Second, what should society do in respect of these consequences? Utilitarianism provides ready answers to both questions. In relation to the first question, classical utilitarians emphasise pleasure and the absence of pain. In answer to the second question, they favour the greatest amount of pleasure all told.[1] There are, of course, well-known advantages and disadvantages with utilitarian ethics. But rather than getting into the hoary debate between those who believe that utilitarianism offers a very practical morality and gets to the heart of what people really care about and those who believe instead that it is merely dogmatic and has morally abhorrent implications, I wish to concentrate on what utilitarianism might tell us about personal responsibility.

To this end, consider the issue of whether or not a society committed to utilitarianism should redistribute money from the rich to the poor. At first glance, it seems that a utilitarian society should support a policy of brute redistribution. This is because money has diminishing marginal utility: the more money people have, the less pleasure they derive from additional amounts of it. So it is sensible to take money from the rich and give it to the poor. A more sophisticated utilitarian analysis of this issue, however, would also take account of the utility-enhancing consequences of personal responsibility. For one thing, taxing the financial rewards paid to talented individuals, and thereby ignoring any responsibility they might have for their earnings, may lessen their incentive to work hard and as a result lower rates of economic efficiency, innovation and growth, which may in turn diminish overall utility. Furthermore, requiring persons to

gain access to income through paid employment might actually increase net utility: directly through the greater prosperity
of persons who take up work and the satisfaction they derive
from earning their own keep; indirectly from an increase in the
labour supply and reductions in social exclusion and crime. For
these reasons, a sophisticated utilitarian might support policies
of low taxation and work requirements for those seeking state
support.[2]

SELF-RESPECT

Another part of the attraction of social policies which promote personal responsibility is the enhancement of people's self-respect.
Self-respect is not something governments can simply give to
people like money or housing. It is a positive feeling, sense, or
impression that one has of oneself. It has a psychological standing but also an evaluative component. To lack self-respect can be
to measure oneself against the sort of person one desires to be
and judge that one has come up short. Not only do our interac-
tions with other people partly define the standards of merit by
which we measure ourselves, but they also offer a constant test of
whether or not we have lived up to those standards. Public shame
occurs when our failure to live up to standards is made common
knowledge.[3]

The connection between personal responsibility and the social
bases of self-respect can take many forms but is often presented
in terms of access to employment. It is commonly argued that
through paid employment individuals gain a level of self-respect
they might not otherwise achieve. One can gain self-respect
through an awareness of one's mastery in a job well done as con-
firmed by the fact that others think it worthwhile to pay an income.
What is more, to earn a wage and pay one's own way; to succeed
in securing one's own long-term future; to develop and successfully pursue an occupational ambition; to increase one's skills and

move up the employment ladder – these are all things that can enhance one's evaluation of oneself as a person with merit.

Now it would be wrong to claim that paid employment is the only way to promote self-respect. Being good at a hobby or even at unpaid work can have a similar effect. But it remains the case that paid employment is an important source of self-respect for many millions of people. Sometimes people who find themselves out of work offer the excuse that if other individuals can't be bothered to work for a living then why should they. The argument from self-respect pulls the rug from under this excuse. Non-compliance on the part of other similarly situated people does not lessen the fact that working produces positive benefits for the individual.

The idea that the state must secure not only personal liberty and the mechanisms of income and wealth but also the social bases of self-respect is a distinctive feature of modern liberal thought. This is due in large measure to the influence of Rawls' iconic book, *A Theory of Justice*. He argues that the social bases of self-respect are perhaps the most important 'primary goods' of life and that the basic institutions of society have a significant role to play in providing these bases.[4] One way to do this is to ensure a distribution of income and wealth that makes people feel that other members of society recognise them as equally important members and are even willing to make sacrifices to ensure that the position of the worst off is improved. However, in his later work Rawls placed particular emphasis on the link between paid employment and self-respect. So great is the importance of the social bases of self-respect in modern liberal societies that if jobs are not readily available in the private sector, then jobs should be created in local government for this purpose.[5]

Having said that paid employment can be a source of self-respect, I must now qualify the argument in three ways. The first qualification is that not all jobs are better for people's self-respect than no job at all. The case of prostitution provides one of a number of possible counter-examples to any simple generalisation. Even people working in perfectly respectable jobs can experience shame and humiliation if the working environment is one of bullying and harassment. So the argument must be that work has the potential to support an important kind of self-respect *provided* that it is of a satisfactory or acceptable standard. This, of course, leaves open the question of what constitutes decent work. It might be thought that someone who flips burgers at McDonald's for minimum wage cannot possibly gain a comparable positive feeling from his work as a doctor or lawyer. This may be true. But the more pressing comparison is with someone who remains unemployed. Some social research looking at poor inner city areas in the US shows that even poorly paid routine labour has positive benefits for self-esteem as well as for social networking and self-discipline.[6]

The second qualification is that there are dangers in building up expectations of work that cannot be fulfilled. Making access to welfare benefits conditional on accepting a place on a training programme isn't necessarily a bad thing. But when the government starts making unrealistic promises about what a training programme will give someone, such as a great job at the end of the training period, this might be a way of setting people up for a fall. Of course, providing education or training for people identified as having low skills might be the first step on the road to employment and with it self-respect. But for some people, the first step along the road could prove to be their only step.

A third qualification concerns the process of identifying people as having shortfalls in aptitude or talent in the first place. Any system that attempts to uphold choice and mitigate brute luck must try to distinguish between those who choose not to work and those who are unable to work because they lack the talents required by employers. But this carries with it the risk of damaging the self-respect of those who must submit to such assessments. How can people maintain their sense of self-worth if they are forced to disclose things about themselves in public which they find shameful? Jonathan Wolff dubs this the problem of 'shameful revelation'. The problem is that in trying to promote fairness and self-respect for some individuals, the state might fail to treat other people with due respect. According to some philosophers, one of the main benefits of unconditional basic income, in contrast to making access to social assistance conditional on attending interviews or job-seeking behaviour, is that it avoids the problem of shameful revelation.[7]

AUTONOMY

Another reason for valuing personal responsibility is that it involves the exercise of autonomy. Consider once again Rawls' contention that in a just society it is the responsibility of the individual to adjust his or her personal tastes and preferences over time to the share of resources he or she can reasonably expect to receive. It has been suggested that this adjustment is not merely a matter of fairness to others but also a part of a good life, a facet of autonomy. If learning to revise one's personal ends to better suit one's budget or else to delay gratification is bound up with the exercise of our autonomy, then for the state to subsidise expensive tastes would be morally unwelcome.[8]

The argument from autonomy is not exhausted by the example of expensive tastes. In the case of poverty and access to social welfare those on the political right often argue that dependency on the state is as bad for dependants as it is for taxpayers. The claim is that deciding how best to respond to poverty should be left to persons who find themselves in that situation and not decided by welfare officials. Likewise, in the arena of health it is increasingly argued that individuals should have the autonomy to decide how much, if any, of their income to spend on healthcare, including medical insurance, and that to force individuals to pay into compulsory insurance schemes is a violation of that autonomy. The danger here is that individuals will be compelled to live their lives in accordance with social standards as to what a 'healthy life' means – a form of health tyranny.[9]

Another autonomy-based argument highlights the intimate connection between the act of choosing and the consequences that follow. Assume for the sake of argument that making a choice is intrinsically a good thing – one aspect of what makes us human. One important part of choosing is taking into consideration the different consequences that might result from our choices. Since the act of choosing must include some consideration as to the possible consequences, it would be wrong to allow the agent to avoid those consequences. To do so would make his choice quite empty.[10]

A more pragmatic argument is that without the intimate connection between choices and consequences individuals tend to get careless. If, for example, the state assumes responsibility for people's medical treatment across the board and without question, it removes the link between conduct and consequence and so effectively removes personal responsibility for ill-health. Where individuals lack the incentive to make prudent self-regarding choices about their own health, over time they lose the capacity to do so and are more likely to make unwise choices and become unwell. This is an argument from moral hazard.

Additional answers can be found in the work of Hart and Scanlon. One clear advantage of living in a society where what happens to us depends on the choices we make is that this gives us a powerful tool for predicting what will happen in the future, thereby allowing us to make long-term plans. Another advantage is that it offers a mechanism by which individuals can get what they want and avoid what they don't want. In the sphere of production and consumption it is now widely accepted that the market is a useful mechanism because it enables large numbers of people to realise many of their desires. So why should access to health and housing be any different? A related advantage of connecting choices with consequences is that such a regime enables us to communicate to others – in a world where it is generally understood that consequences are attached to choices – what we value and cherish. Even more importantly, being denied the opportunity to have what happens to us depend on the choices we make could be symbolic of the fact that we are considered somehow incapable of looking after ourselves. Other things remaining equal we want authorities to adopt policies that treat us as autonomous beings are competent to be left in charge of our own lives.[11]

There are, however, limits to the value of autonomy. First, the exercise of choice is not without cost for the individual – in terms of time and energy in gathering and assessing information and the anxiety associated with 'making the right choice'. So there may come a point at which the burden of having to make a choice is greater than the benefit of having the right to choose. Second, some goods are such that what matters to us is not that we have the choice but that we get the outcome we want. For example, do patients really care about being able to choose their own hospital provided that they get a good operation? Third, that choices are linked to consequences is by no means the only form of self-expression that people care about. Fourth, when it comes to access to food, shelter and life-saving medical treatment it may be that paternalism is not so disrespectful after all. After all, one reason why it might be right for the government to break the link between choices and consequences when it comes to access to these basic necessities is that they are vital for protecting the exercise of autonomy in the future.

Of course, at this stage in the argument a libertarian might insist that it is morally insupportable for the state to shield persons from the consequences of their autonomous choices. If autonomy is valuable, then people should have a protected sphere of activity, including activity which is very likely to harm the agent. Nevertheless, accepting the value of autonomy does not entail an absolute right to non-interference. It is perfectly consistent with the idea of a protected sphere of personal activity to have limits to that protected sphere. Arguably it is morally fitting to use some degree of state intervention to ensure that people enjoy the capacity for autonomous action over the entire course of their lives. None of this is intended to demonstrate that libertarians are necessarily mistaken. Rather, the point is that appealing to the value of autonomy does not by itself justify libertarian rights.

HUMAN FLOURISHING

What is particularly disturbing to some people about public dependency is not so much that it is unfair to those on whom individuals depend, but what it says about, and does to, the moral character of the person who is dependent. Autonomy is one part of this but it is not the only part. The Victorians condemned the Poor Laws for fostering a range of vices including intemperance and over-population. In the words of the Reverend Malthus:

> The labouring poor, to use a vulgar expression, seem always to live from hand to mouth. Their present wants employ their whole attention, and they seldom think of the future. Even when they have an opportunity of saving, they seldom exercise it; but all that they earn beyond their present necessities goes, generally speaking, to the alehouse. The poor law may, therefore, be said to diminish both the power and the will to save, among the common people, and thus to weaken one of the strongest incentives to sobriety and industry, and consequently to happiness.[12]

Human flourishing has to do with living a good human life, and the latter is often associated with the presence of virtue and the absence of vice. Some virtues, such as the virtue of self-reliance, are closely related to the idea of taking responsibility for our own welfare. There is, however, a further class of virtues which, although often associated with personal responsibility in that sense, are not strictly necessary for it. Self-discipline, the ability to delay gratification, being hard-working, thrifty, honest – these are all virtues that a person *might* need if he wished to pay his own way in life. But in theory a person could demonstrate a complete lack of such virtues but still assume personal responsibility for the consequences of his actions in an important sense. He could eat, drink and be merry today, knowing that tomorrow he will have nothing, but nevertheless not let himself become a drag on others tomorrow by refusing to ask for assistance. Of course, if he achieved this simply by hiding himself away so that others will not feel guilty by his presence, he may yet be committing the vice of pride.

Aside from virtue and vice, there are plenty of other instances in moral discourse where 'good' is identified with *what comes naturally*. It is often said that a life of idleness is not a natural life, for example. The social commentator J. A. Hobson articulated this line of thought rather well when in 1902 he wrote that 'Nature imposes the obligation of work as a condition of enjoyment, and it belongs to a well-ordered society to enforce this obligation.'[13] The idea that useful labour is a natural disposition, one that is subverted by social welfare provision, can also be found in more recent political texts. The 1979 Conservative Party election manifesto contains the following example: 'We want to work with the grain of human nature, helping people to help themselves – and others. This is the way to restore that self-reliance and self-confidence which are the basis of personal responsibility and national success.'

The suggestion is that human beings naturally rely on their own powers to meet their needs; they forage, hunt, produce or else trade their talents in order to obtain the resources they need to survive; they decide how, and when, to do these things and what degree of effort will be required and for how long. Hence, to be dependent on others is to confound one's own nature. This account of what comes *naturally* to human beings, however, is far from uncontroversial. All human beings must at some point in their lives depend on others, whether as children or elderly persons, or when sick and injured. Even the act of trading with other people is a dependency of sorts. So the attempt to construe welfare dependency as unnatural can be problematic.

Plus the foregoing account of human nature is by no means the only account on the table. Karl Marx, for example, emphasised the sociality of human nature. He argued that through the workers' revolution a new social order would come into existence which substitutes the self-oriented and class-stratified system of capitalistic production with a new 'social bond' characterised by relations of cooperative joint production and shared ownership. No doubt some people will insist that Marx's vision simply replaces mutual exploitation with a system of mutual dependency; neither of which capture genuine human flourishing. But it is clear that for Marx human flourishing and mutual cooperation are bound together.[14] Furthermore, an important strain of feminist scholarship emphasises the fact that there is an inevitable and not necessarily regrettable human dependency which both conservatives and liberal egalitarians have ignored. Feminists argue that thinkers like Rawls labour under the myth of independent moral agents who are not born, do not develop under the care of their parents, never get sick, are not disabled and do not grow old.[15]

There is much that could be said both about these alternative perspectives on human dependency and in defence of Rawls. But my aim here is not to settle the dispute concerning what is the best account of human flourishing and of human nature. Even without the controversial assumption that human beings are naturally non-dependent creatures, there are grounds for thinking that personal responsibility is an important feature of human flourishing. Indeed, while some forms of personal responsibility might be contrary to the ideals of a socialist society, other forms play a vital role in its main ethos. For example, if personal responsibility means being able to get extremely rich off the back of one's own talents or taking care of oneself independently of collective action, then this is ruled out under socialism. But if personal responsibility means not taking advantage of the benefits of collective action without giving something in return, then personal responsibility is central to the socialist ethic.

NATURAL DUTIES AND SPECIAL OBLIGATIONS

Yet another way in which personal responsibility can be seen as being part of the moral fabric of our lives is through the idea that assuming responsibility is a moral duty of all healthy adults. One version of this argument can be found in the moral theory of the seventeenth-century philosopher John Locke. Locke believed that each person has a moral duty to support himself through work wherever possible. This duty is owed not to kings, or even to fellow citizens, but to God. He argued that since our continued existence is due to God, we owe a duty to preserve our lives in a way that God intends, and God intends healthy adults to work on the land and be self-reliant. How do we know this is what God intends? Locke thought that the natural ends or purposes intended for humanity are writ large in the nature of things and are discoverable by human reason. To be more specific, Locke held that it would contradict the idea of a wise Creator to suppose that human beings, who are blessed with the capacity for useful labour, are not obligated to make good use of this capacity. Consequently, Locke believed that for those who are not elderly, sick or disabled, the true and proper relief of poverty consists in setting the idle to work.[16]

These arguments are anachronistic by today's standards. Nowadays it is thought that the state should offer the idle every opportunity to work and may use economic sanctions against individuals who refuse these opportunities. Few people seriously think that the state should lock the idle up in workhouses. Furthermore, Locke's justification for the natural duty to work for a living is based on a religious view of human nature and how we ought to live. In contrast to this, many contemporary liberals affirm that governments must endeavour to meet the test of 'justificatory neutrality': the justifications they offer for state intervention must not be based on controversial assumptions about human nature and the good life – assumptions based on a particular religious doctrine, for example – since such things have a tendency to divide rather than unite citizens, and call into question the legitimacy of the state.[17]

So what else could ground the moral imperative to take personal responsibility? In some cases it might be appropriate to speak not of *natural duties* but of the *special obligations* that persons have to the government or to the rest of society. Consider, for example, a scheme whereby people who wish to receive unemployment benefits are invited to sign a contract in which they agree to meet with welfare officials at regular intervals to discuss future employment and to improve their job-seeking behaviour. If they sign the contract, then we can say that the person has an obligation to assume personal responsibility. This piggybacks on a more general obligation to honour our commitments.

This sort of argument, however, invites the following obvious question: why should people agree to make such commitments in the first place? At this point it is possible to draw once again on some of the reasons mentioned above and in the previous chapter. But this isn't strictly necessary. One reason why people might sign up to these agreements is if they can be persuaded by good caseworkers that it is in their best interests to do so. If the fact of the matter is that persons who refuse to sign up are more likely to remain in poverty than those who do, this provides a ready motivation for individuals to sign. Indeed, if other people are foolish enough not to sign, this might improve their prospects still further, since there is less competition for the available jobs.

A MATTER OF PERSPECTIVES?

Thus far I have framed the debate in terms of a plurality of moral reasons for caring about personal responsibility. Another way of framing the debate prevalent in the literature on social policy is in terms of the distinction between backward-looking and forward-looking perspectives. The backward-looking perspective tends to focus on the causes of misfortune. Here the question is

'Why should society help people who are responsible for their own downfalls?' Indeed, this is the question posed by the ants in Aesop's fable quoted at the start of Chapter 1. 'What did you do this past summer?' ask the ants. In contrast to this, the forward-looking perspective considers what can be done to improve people's behaviour in the future. Here the question is, 'What can society do to foster a greater sense of personal responsibility among people in the future?' In some cases withholding assistance makes it nigh-on impossible for individuals to behave more responsibly in the future. If the ants don't agree to help the grasshopper, then he will probably starve to death and the ants will be unable to impress upon him the importance of working hard during the summer. Of course, the ants might say that they are making an example of the grasshopper to deter others. But arguably that is to treat the grasshopper as a means to end and not as an end himself.

The distinction between backward- and forward-looking perspectives also comes to the fore in the context of healthcare. To adopt the backward-looking perspective is to view personal responsibility as a criterion for determining whether or not people should be entitled to treatment given the causes of their ill-health. Persons who are deemed to be 'at fault' for their illnesses may forfeit their right to treatment. This perspective is much maligned. But the reasons for its unpopularity are complex. Some people seem to think that few individuals *really are* responsible for their own ill-health. Others think that this sort of treatment is contrary to the principles of compassion and treatment-according-to-need which ought to underpin healthcare. The forward-looking perspective, by contrast, takes a view about where we are tying to get to in relation to the distribution of health and healthcare and as a result focuses on how to encourage individuals to be more responsible in the future. So, for example, we might support a system of cash bonuses or rebates on insurance premiums paid to people who change their behaviour with regard to smoking, diet and exercise.

Although the distinction between backward- and forward-looking perspectives can be helpful in some cases, it also needs to be handled with caution. One reason for caution is that the justification for a forward-looking policy can sometimes depend on a backward-looking argument. For instance, we might want people to stop smoking in the future partly because we think that smokers should be held responsible for the consequences of their actions, and we want to avoid a situation where we have to impose backward-looking responsibility. A further reason is that it can be unclear how to describe a particular policy. If the ants refuse to help the grasshopper, for example, there is a sense in which this is a backward-looking policy. But suppose they do this in order to make an example of him, so that other grasshoppers will sit up and take notice. If so, then there is a sense in which this is a forward-looking policy, just not for this particular grasshopper.

A third reason for caution is that the choice of perspectives is itself not a neutral choice. The following example illustrates this point. In 1996 President Clinton made an executive order mandating that young mothers receiving welfare benefits should sign a 'personal responsibility agreement' promising to remain living with their parents and to stay in school. On the surface, it might seem that asking these girls to behave as directed is a way of undermining personal responsibility. It draws out the period of dependency on parents and shuns the responsibility associated with bringing up one's own children, living under one's own roof and working for a living. Some defenders of the policy, however, argued that there is an alternative way of seeing this agreement, namely, as something that puts these young women in a better position to take personal responsibility for themselves and for their children in the longer term. This may be entirely reasonable. Nevertheless, the defenders of this policy must explain why this is a good thing, why it is right to adopt the more forward-looking perspective.

Although there are no hard and fast connections between

the two perspectives and the moral reasons discussed in this chapter, it is possible to make some rough generalisations. So, for example, people who are attracted to the backward-looking perspective are often motivated by considerations of fairness alone, whereas the forward-looking perspective tends to attract the attention of people who are motivated by a much wider set of ethical concerns, such as the desire to promote human flourishing. This implies that if we value personal responsibility not simply because of fairness but also because we think it is a good way of life for people to lead, then sometimes it might be better to waive personal responsibility now, so that persons are better able to assume responsibility at a later date. It seems to me that this line of thought holds the key to understanding a great many disagreements within social policy, and it is something to which I shall return in Chapter 7. But notice that what is doing the work here is not merely a distinction between two different perspectives but crucially a distinction between different underlying values.

COMBINING VALUES

In Chapters 3 and 4 I have outlined a number of reasons for thinking that personal responsibility matters: fairness, utility, self-respect, autonomy, human flourishing, natural duty and special obligation. I don't claim that this list is exhaustive. No doubt other reasons could have been added. Yet it is more than enough to be getting along with.

So what now? The difficulty of putting this list of values into practice can be illustrated with the example of unemployment and public dependency. While some conceptions of fairness would refuse public assistance to people who are voluntarily unemployed – assuming that such people can be identified – other conceptions favour an unconditional basic income for all. Utilitarianism may not condemn public dependency per se, but it will condemn public dependency should it reduce net utility. Respect for autonomy implies that it would be a good thing for individuals to take control of their own lives by working for a living. But it also implies that the state must respect people's voluntary choices. So if an adult wants to lead a life of idle leisure and fully appreciates the implications of this choice, respect for autonomy implies that he or she should have less residual income as a consequence but also that no undue influence should be heaped on his or her decision. The values of self-respect and human flourishing, by contrast, might support policies designed to hassle individuals back into work if that is for their own good. On the assumption that we value all of these things to some degree, which policies should we favour?

It might be argued at this stage that if only I had been more discriminating in compiling the above list of values it wouldn't be so unmanageable. But this response is rather too hasty. For it relies on the questionable assumption that smaller lists do not attract the problem of value conflict. The truth is otherwise. I offer two illustrations.

Having previously championed equality of opportunity for welfare, Arneson now defends what he calls 'responsibility-catering prioritarianism'. It states that the right policy is the one that maximises people's welfare, with two stipulations. First, increases in welfare are more important the lower the person's welfare prior to receipt of the benefit. Second, increases in welfare are less important the greater a person's degree of responsibility for his position prior to receipt of the benefit.[18] But Arneson does not pause to stipulate how much weight should be given to the various elements of his theory. As a result, there are weaker and stronger interpretations. A strong interpretation says that *any* additional weight given to gains to the welfare of those who are very badly off is undone by choice and responsibility, meaning that gains to the welfare of someone who is very badly off will count the same as gains to the welfare of someone who is more advantaged if both are equally responsible for their positions.

A weaker interpretation says that only some of the additional weight given to gains to the welfare of the very badly off is lost through choice, so that gains to the welfare of someone who is very badly off will still count for slightly more than gains to the welfare of someone who is more advantaged even if both are equally responsible for their positions. But how much more?

For his part, Wolff insists that any attempt to make social welfare policies fairer must be sensitive to the problem of shameful revelation in the case of claimants who lack the talents necessary to command economic rent. But faced with the question of how, more exactly, to balance the two requirements of fairness and respect, Wolff simply states that 'legislators should legislate in a way that allows flexibility'. In effect, Wolff cannot say for sure what the exact weighting of the two requirements should be. Instead, legislators should give welfare officials or administrators the leeway to crack down on bogus claimants in some circumstances but be more lenient and sensitive to the needs of genuine claimants in other circumstances, presumably in line with cycles of economic growth and decline.[19]

The point of these two examples is to show that even relatively small lists of values can be indeterminate with respect to their best weighting.

It might be argued that there is no genuine problem here because policymakers may prefer to have a menu of possibilities from which to choose. Policymakers wish to know which of the various policies on the table could be justified. They can then use other practical considerations to narrow down the field. Now I don't deny that having a menu of possibilities may be useful in some contexts. Nevertheless, there is such a thing as sitting on the fence and if philosophers wish to be more helpful, then this is something they ought not to do. For suppose a policymaker already has an idea of what is practically possible but simply wishes to have some guidance on whether to choose policy A or B. If the philosopher tells him or her that there is simply no truth of the matter which is better, since both A and B realise important values in reasonable ways, then the policymaker might be forgiven for feeling a little frustrated by this advice.

If, in contrast to this, philosophers were able to provide policymakers with a set of rules or principles for determining the relative importance of different values, it might help to narrow down the range of policies. Assuming it is possible to rank values in order of importance A, B, C, D and so on, policymakers could select policies which satisfy value A, then if there are any choices still to be made they could select policies which satisfy B, then C, D and so on. Or else philosophers could try to develop a more sophisticated weighting system bringing in real numbers between a range of 0 to 10 (say) representing the cardinal values of the relevant values. Or perhaps they could establish a set of ordinal functions for pairs of values such as A > B, B > C, and C > A. Policymakers could then aim to make divisions between social and personal responsibility which satisfy all the given functions.

The obvious problem is how to arrive at a list of rankings or functions. Although I think that it is right to try to develop more and more sophisticated accounts of the relative importance of the values in play, I am also dubious as to whether philosophers can complete this task alone. It seems to me that the sorts of rankings or pairings that are required are more aptly produced through a direct dialogue between philosophers, policymakers, politicians and ordinary citizens. In other words, the sense of reasonableness required is likely to call for the intuitions and nuanced judgements of people from all of these groups. I shall offer my account of how this might be done in Chapter 8.

5   What Do Politicians Think?

Our vision is of a high skills, high productivity, high employment economy based on the principles of strong enterprise and social justice. A society where more opportunities, and more choices, are matched by a greater responsibility on the part of individuals to help themselves.

Tony Blair

The idea of personal responsibility is now very much on the political agenda. Politicians regularly evoke the idea to make their case for reform of the welfare state, for changes to public sector health services and for the improvement of society in general. In doing so they draw on assumptions about human motivation along with empirical claims about social and economic conditions seasoned with various forms of popular thinking, and some not so subtle electioneering of course. But scratch beneath the surface and it is not hard to find versions of many of the principles and values discussed in Chapters 3 and 4. Politicians are not averse to drawing on moral and political philosophy to make arguments about why personal responsibility matters. The idea of balancing rights and responsibilities is dominant in Britain at the moment and is a case in point: for it appears to be an argument of fairness. The purpose of this chapter is to map out the political terrain on personal responsibility and to render more explicit the different kinds of moral arguments that stand behind the different kinds of political rhetoric.

A BRIEF TYPOLOGY

I begin with a description of the main forces within British political life and what they have to say about personal responsibility. Historically those on the left have argued that bringing social welfare provision under the collective control of the state is crucial for equality and solidarity. This is not to say that shortfalls on the side of personal responsibility do not matter. The left believe that to take advantage of the benefits of collective action without giving something in return is not merely exploitative but also a threat to social unity. In the 1945 general election, for example, Clement Attlee's Labour Party defeated Winston Churchill's Conservatives less than three months after Churchill had announced the Nazi surrender. Attlee's government promised the British people more food, more employment, more housing and social insurance against a rainy day. But the important point was that these benefits were to be achieved through collective action and reciprocal cooperation – the winning manifesto declared that the 'Labour Party is a socialist party and proud of it'.

By contrast, the political right in Britain has tended to promote personal responsibility both as a way of creating material prosperity for individuals and their families and as an essential ingredient of a good human life in the larger sense. While the preservation of human life might call for the relief of severe poverty and the reduction of unemployment, the right believe that the best mechanisms for achieving those ends are more likely to be found in the private and voluntary sectors than in state intervention. What is more, personal responsibility is a moral good, an end in itself. During the 1980s, for example, Margaret Thatcher argued that the welfare state erodes the virtues of hard work and self-reliance, which, in her view, are constituent features of a flourishing life. The idea that the welfare state creates a 'dependency culture' and weakens the moral fibre of the working man was summed up in the iconic story told by

Norman Tebbit about his own father, who every morning 'got on his bike' and looked for work.

The electoral success of New Labour during the 1990s and early 2000s owed much to its distancing itself from its old socialist aims. By convincing the Labour Party to abandon Clause IV of its constitution – which called for 'the common ownership of the means of production' – Tony Blair was able to reach out to the voters of middle England. Many people had had enough of Thatcher's harsh socio-economic policies. Blair's Third Way sought to combine together elements of both left-wing and right-wing economic and political thinking. But it did not always do so in clear and consistent ways. The Third Way at times emphasises the need for collective action in tackling social deprivation, which in turn helps to create social cohesion and solidarity, at other times underscores personal responsibility as a traditional British value, and on still other occasions claims that it is unfair for citizens to expect 'something for nothing'.

For his part, David Cameron has his eyes set on becoming the next British Prime Minister. His particular brand of modern Conservatism seeks to dispel two misnomers. The first misnomer is that the Conservative Party is a libertarian party – a party which believes that freedom is the be all and end all. According to Cameron, the most important word in politics is 'responsibility' rather than 'freedom'.[1] (There are parallels here with Blair's removal of the socialist Clause IV.) In January 2006 he established the Social Justice Policy Group to make recommendations to the Tories on how to tackle Britain's social problems. Its 2007 report, *Breakthrough Britain*, encapsulates his thinking: 'Our approach is based on the belief that people must take responsibility for their own choices but that government has a responsibility to help people make the right choices.'[2]

The emphasis on 'the right choices' is connected with the second misnomer, namely, that it is inappropriate for politicians to be judgemental about personal behaviour. 'We as a society have been far too sensitive,' claims Cameron.

In order to avoid injury to people's feelings, in order to avoid appearing judgemental, we have failed to say what needs to be said. We have seen a decades-long erosion of responsibility, of social virtue, of self-discipline, respect for others, deferring gratification instead of instant gratification. Our relationships crack up, our marriages break down, we fail as parents and as citizens just like everyone else. But if the result of this is a stultifying silence about things that really matter, we re-double the failure. Refusing to use these words – right and wrong – means a denial of personal responsibility and the concept of a moral choice. We talk about people being 'at risk of obesity' instead of talking about people who eat too much and take too little exercise. We talk about people being at risk of poverty, or social exclusion: it's as if these things – obesity, alcohol abuse, drug addiction – are purely external events like a plague or bad weather. Of course, circumstances – where you are born, your neighbourhood, your school, and the choices your parents make – have a huge impact. But social problems are often the consequence of the choices that people make.[3]

This means that the idea of personal responsibility is functioning in different, almost mirrored ways in Blair and Cameron's discourse. For Blair, the emphasis on personal responsibility was about fairness. He needed to persuade the taxpayers of middle England that he was not going to let welfare scroungers sponge off them. For Cameron, personal responsibility has more to do with visions of a good life and fixing our broken society. His task is to convince centrist voters – many of whom supported Blair during the 1990s – that encouraging individuals to assume ever greater personal responsibility for their own lives is not merely a more effective way of improving their life chances than through state intervention but also the right way to live.

What I find most interesting about Cameron's discourse is the explicit rejection of the test of neutrality which underpins a good deal of contemporary liberal egalitarian philosophy. Many of the thinkers discussed in Chapter 3 believe that a liberal government should not attempt to justify policies on the grounds that one conception of the good life is better than another. They are attracted to the principle of choice and responsibility – that it is fitting to hold people responsible for the consequences of their voluntary choices – precisely because it seems to be a way of assigning consequential responsibility without making controversial judgements about whether one kind of lifestyle is better or worse, or more or less deserving, than another. Of course, it might be countered that assignments of consequential responsibility are at their best precisely when they do make such judgements. Nevertheless, I think that the moral tone of Cameron's rhetoric shows that he is not troubled by the test of neutrality. He is content to be a moral perfectionist.

INTERNATIONAL COMPARISONS

No typology would be complete, however, without looking at the international dimension. Thatcher, of course, was greatly influenced by the arguments of the New Right in the US and by her close relationship with Ronald Reagan. During the 1980s thinkers of the New Right argued that welfare programmes such as Aid to Families with Dependent Children (AFDC) only served to help women have more children than they could afford to support and succeeded in eroding among the poorest sections of American society the principles of hard work, individual initiative and self-reliance.[4] Reagan used the label 'Cadillac queens' to describe women who could even afford to drive luxury cars because of the generous benefits they received from the government. Many of Thatcher's views on welfare reform mirrored Reagan's belief that the ultimate success of welfare should be judged by how many of its recipients become welfare independent.

In a move designed to gain the ground on welfare reform Bill Clinton promised 'to end welfare as we know it' during his 1992 presidential campaign. He achieved his ambitions in August 1996 when the US Congress passed the Personal Responsibility and

Work Opportunity Reconciliation Act. Congress replaced AFDC with Temporary Assistance for Needy Families (TANF) which included a five-year lifetime limit for receiving cash assistance and required single mothers to seek paid employment. Shortly after that in 1997 Gordon Brown went on a fact-finding mission to the US to investigate Clinton's welfare reforms. Although the Labour government didn't fully replicate the fixed cut-off strategy, Brown's first budget as Chancellor of the Exchequer in 1997 included a reduction of benefits for lone parents. This didn't play well with the Party, however, as 120 Labour MPs wrote to Brown challenging the cuts and 47 actually voted against the government. Although the government ultimately defeated an opposition motion, this was the first major revolt of the New Labour era.

Of course, Labour politicians are not alone in trying to defend social policies on the basis of 'what works' in the US. Cameron has praised the welfare reforms of the former Republican Governor of Wisconsin, Tommy Thompson, who during his 14 years in office was able to dramatically cut the number of dependent families or 'caseload'.[5] Speaking at the Conservative Party conference in 2007, Cameron offered the following argument: 'In states like Wisconsin in America where they've cut benefit rolls by 80 per cent, and the changes we will make are these: we will say to people that if you are offered a job and it's a fair job and one that you can do and you refuse it you shouldn't get any welfare.'[6] Yet Cameron's analogy obscures an important difference between the US and Britain. In the US there is not only a strong tradition of self-reliance but also a widespread practice of charitable giving. The Governor of Wisconsin was able to rely on a strong voluntary sector to pick up the slack when people no longer had access to cash from the state but remained unemployed. To be sure, Cameron would like ordinary British citizens to get more involved in philanthropic activity. But this may be unrealistic. A survey undertaken by the Salvation Army in 2003, for example, found that 79 per cent of respondents in Britain agreed with the proposition that charities are currently having to fund many of the basic social services that should be provided by the government.[7]

The new US President, Barack Obama, looks set to rekindle Clinton's strategy of combining state support for the poorest citizens with a greater emphasis on personal responsibility for 'ordinary folk'. In July 2008, for example, Obama told the National Association for the Advancement of Colored People (NAACP) that as well as demanding more responsibility from Washington and Wall Street, African Americans must demand more respon-sibility from themselves.[8] This was in spite of Jesse Jackson's criticism that he had overemphasised the responsibility of African Americans and not said enough about lack of equal opportunity. Obama returned to this theme during his acceptance speech for the Democratic nomination in August 2008. He told the National Convention:

> Democrats, we must also admit that fulfilling America's promise will require more than just money. It will require a renewed sense of responsibility from each of us to recover what John F. Kennedy called our "intellectual and moral strength." . . . Individual responsibility and mutual responsibility – that's the essence of America's promise.[9]

So there are significant moves on both sides of the Atlantic to underscore personal responsibility alongside social provision for the most vulnerable people in society. However, what is the level of political support for the proposal, discussed in Chapter 3, for an unconditional basic income, sometimes called a 'citi-zen's income', funded by taxpayers and payable to every citizen whether or not they are in work? While it is hard to gauge momentum, there is undoubtedly modest support for uncondi-tional basic income by academics, political activists and politi-cians around the world. Tommy Thompson, for example, has endorsed unconditional basic income as part of the strategy for rebuilding Iraq. Namibia's basic income proposal has received praise from the UN Commission for Social Development. And in 2004 the Citizen's Income Trust conducted a survey of British MPs and of the 71 completed questionnaires and 11 letters returned, 41 respondents were in favour and 11 against.[10]

Nevertheless, there are cautionary tales for those politicians thinking about running on a basic income ticket in major elections. In the 1972 US presidential campaign the Democratic Party's candidate George McGovern proposed a 'demogrant' for the American people but was overwhelmingly defeated by the incumbent President, Richard Nixon. John McDonnell, MP for the Australian Labour Party, failed in his 2006 leadership campaign having endorsed a citizen's income. The winner of that leadership contest, Kevin Rudd, made no such commitment and went on to become the Prime Minister of Australia in the 2007 general election. The Green Party of England and Wales champions the citizen's income as a way of helping people escape the 'poverty trap'. Although the Party has some members in the European Parliament, the London Assembly and in local government, it is unrepresented in the House of Commons. Of course, it does not follow from this that McGovern and McDonnell lost because of their support for unconditional basic income or that the Green Party is unrepresented in the House of Commons for the same reason. But it is still the case that advocacy of unconditional basic income is hitherto the preserve of politicians and parties who end up on the losing side in major elections.

In what follows I return to the case of Britain and try to unpack current political thinking in the two key areas of social welfare and healthcare reform.

WELFARE REFORM

Not long after Tony Blair swept to office in 1997 he appointed Frank Field as the Minister for Welfare Reform with a brief to 'think the unthinkable'. Field set out his thoughts in a Green Paper entitled, *New Ambitions for Our Country: A New Contract for Welfare*. 'At the heart of the modern welfare state will be a new contract

between the citizen and the government, based on responsibilities and rights.'[11] What Field gave with one hand, however,
he took away with the other. He proposed to restrict the use of
means-tested benefits, thereby allowing those with disabilities
the chance to work without the fear of losing their benefits. But at
the same time he proposed tougher medical tests for new claimants. He suggested that as many as two-thirds of claimants for
disability benefits did not have sufficient supporting evidence.

Field was asked to think the unthinkable, but ultimately his
political masters decided that he had thought up the wrong kind
of unthinkable. Brown went ahead with proposals for means-
tested tax credits, which caused yet more backbench unrest.
Blair's response to this situation came in July 1998 when he
replaced Harriet Harman with Alistair Darling as Secretary of State
for Social Security. Field, who had expected to be given the top
job, resigned from his post. In a vinegary resignation statement
Field blamed the welfare policy standoff on Brown, claiming that
Brown had, in effect, sabotaged his agenda for welfare reform
despite Blair's support. In an interview published in the *Daily Mail*
a few days later, Brown hit back saying that he could not support
Field's proposals because they would have involved 'billions of
pounds of extra taxes'.[12]

Nevertheless, one important aspect of Fields' reforms has
remained intact, and that is the core principle of 'workfare': that
as a condition of receiving welfare benefits there should be an
expectation of work or training for those who can work or train.
Jobcentre Plus offices have been at the vanguard of delivering
these work requirements in Britain. They began to operate coun-
trywide in 2002 offering access to both Jobseeker's Allowance
and employment services. The rationale is that if Jobcentre Plus
agents can actively procure work or job training on behalf of
claimants, and require them to accept these opportunities as a
precondition of receiving benefits, then people will be unemployed for a shorter period of time. As Alistair Darling puts it:
'When people come through the door – they will no longer simply

be able to ask: "What can you pay out to me?" They will have to answer the question: "What can we do to help you into a job?"[13]

One justification offered for this policy is paternalistic. The government could not have made this justification any clearer than in the title of its 2007 Green Paper, *In Work, Better Off: Next Steps to Full Employment*. But making people better off financially can't be the only justification: for there are always going to be individuals whose preference is not to work whether or not being in work is more financially advantageous than being on benefits. For example, they might think that being able to stay at home and look after their children really is more important than being better off financially. So arguably a certain conception of fairness is also playing a role here: that it is somehow fairer to taxpayers if welfare recipients actively look for work. Thus, in the foreword to *In Work, Better Off*, Peter Hain writes that 'it reinforces our strong commitment to the values of equality and opportunity, and to the principle of rights matched by responsibilities, with work for those who can and security for those who can't.[14] This way of thinking was crystallised in the Welfare Reform Act 2007. Among the new measures it brought into UK law was the requirement that people who are able to work must attend work-focused interviews as a condition of receiving Jobseeker's Allowance.[15]

Lone parents have often been at the sharp end of welfare reform. In an attempt to once again think the unthinkable on welfare reform, Tony Blair appointed David Freud, great-grand-son of Sigmund Freud and experienced city banker, to think about some radical reforms. His report recommended significant increases in the numbers of lone parents moving into paid employment including a plan to require them to seek work when their youngest child reaches the age of 3 or face benefit cuts.[16] These proposals sparked a number of concerns, especially about lone parents with disabled children. Sir Bert Massie, the chairman of the Disability Rights Commission, warned that Freud's proposal risked leaving behind the quarter of lone parents in receipt of welfare benefits who have a disabled child. If lone parents with disabled children are going to re-enter the workplace they need to know that there will be good quality, affordable and accessible childcare and after-school opportunities for their children.[17]

Freud also recommended contracting out some parts of the welfare state to the private sector. The government's initial reaction to this recommendation was lukewarm, but private contractors are now playing an increasing role in the delivery of social welfare and work programmes across Britain. This move, however, raises some interesting ideological questions, such as in the case of existing jobseekers who refuse to cooperate on the principled grounds that they object to such services being provided by profit-driven companies as opposed to agents of social justice. I shall revisit this issue in Chapter 7.

As Prime Minister, Brown has certainly not shied away from this argument. Talking to the BBC's Jon Sopel in January 2008, he summed up the government's new position as follows: 'ten years ago we said look, if you're not prepared to work, we're going to make sure you do work before you get any benefits, you've got to sign up to a condition to work. Now, people will have to sign up to a new condition and the condition is they're prepared to get the skills for work as well. So you can't sit around and do nothing.'[18] In the same month Brown also appointed James Purnell as the new Secretary of State for Work and Pensions, who promptly announced plans that those on Jobseeker's Allowance would be required to carry out four weeks' community work once they have been unemployed for more than a year and after two years may be ordered to work full-time in the community. Not content with that, in December 2008 Brown unveiled plans for future welfare reforms including a requirement that from 2010 lone parents with a youngest child aged 7 will be moved off Income Support and onto Jobseeker's Allowance with a strong expectation of job-seeking and tough sanctions for non-compliance.[19]

Many of these proposals appear in James Purnell's new Welfare Reform Bill 2008–09 which supplements the Welfare Reform Act 2007. Introduced to the House of Commons in January 2009, the

Bill goes one step further on the question of lone parents, so that a lone parent will become a jobseeker as soon as his or her child reaches the age of 3. Echoing the early days of the Labour government in 2007, the Bill has been heavily criticised by Labour backbenchers but nevertheless successfully negotiated its passage through a Public Bill Committee and its final stages in the House of Commons. Just as tough new rules dealing with single parents prompted the first major revolt of the New Labour era, perhaps they prompted one of the final revolts of that era.[20]

In an attempt to reclaim the ground over welfare reform, the Conservatives immediately backed the 'work for benefits' proposals, suggesting that many of the proposals had been theirs first and were borrowed from their policy documents.[21] At the Conservative Party conference in October 2008, Cameron aped the language of New Labour declaring his firm intention to 'end the something for nothing culture.' He explained: 'If you don't take a reasonable offer of a job, you lose benefits. Go on doing it, you'll keep losing benefits. Stay on benefits and you'll have to work for them.'[22] Consistent with this theme, the Conservatives supported the government's Welfare Reform Bill 2008–09 during its passage through the House of Commons in early 2009.

This left the Liberal Democrats, along with a cluster of Labour backbenchers, alone in criticising the Bill. Reiterating many of the concerns raised by Gingerbread, a charity for single parents, the Liberal Democrat Shadow Secretary of State for Work and Pensions, Steve Webb, offered the following response to the Bill. 'The Government clearly regards bringing up young children as a second class activity while we believe that all parents should be able to exercise choice about how they raise their children.'[23]

The idea that persons, including single parents, have an obligation to help themselves through work is not new, of course. But there is another aspect of recent welfare reform that is new. Historically the assumption has been that only able-bodied adults have a duty to work for a living. But now the idea seems to be that virtually everyone has a duty to work except only for the most severely disabled. The Welfare Reform Act 2007 cleared the ground for a number of measures designed to get the disabled into work. Purnell captured the new ethos very well when he said 'my priority is to . . . make the right to work a reality, but also for everybody who can work, to make sure that they all know that they have a responsibility to work'.[24] In October 2008, Incapacity Benefit was replaced with the new Employment and Support Allowance. Claimants will be required to attend a Work Capability Assessment (WCA) designed to determine not only a person's entitlement but also any support he or she needs to get back into the workplace. This new allowance effectively redraws the old distinction between Unemployment Benefits and Incapacity Benefits shifting people who used to be on Incapacity Benefits into a group who must search for work in order to claim. There is a certain irony to this timing as the government seeks to increase the number of jobseekers in a time of economic recession and higher unemployment. Indeed, it was during the economic recessions of the early 1980s and 1990s that many people were put onto Incapacity Benefits as a way of keeping a lid on official unemployment figures.

On the other hand, I suspect that few people would begrudge someone who has a disability or mental health problem the opportunity to be 'in work' if this is something he or she feels able to do and would like to do. For these people interviews may be very helpful, liberating even. According to the government's own research – so far as this can be trusted – between 80 and 90 per cent of those making a new claim to Incapacity Benefit want and expect to return to work in the future.[25] Nevertheless, the problems start when the motivation for the policy shifts from helping people to take responsibility for their own lives to simply getting people off the welfare rolls. Arguably this occurs at the point when people are forced to attend interviews to discuss work or training as a condition of receiving benefits. There are dangers here. Will these measures traduce people who are genuinely unable to work? What is the purpose of punitive measures against disabled claimants whose biggest barrier to employment is still the negative prejudices, ignorance and inflexibility of some employers?

The obsession with work requirements reached its zenith with a proposal by the Housing Minister Caroline Flint that new applicants for social housing should sign 'commitment contracts' pledging to seek employment as a condition of receiving access to housing. In her words, 'Social housing should be based around the principle of something for something.'[26] This raises the question of how far a government may legitimately go in demanding personal responsibility. If local councils have a statutory duty to house homeless families, for example, then what right would councils have to remove people from social housing if they fail to satisfy the terms of their commitment contracts? In other words, does the government have the right to raise the spectre of consequential responsibility in respect of the provision of basic services such as housing?

I shall come back to these questions later in this chapter. But for now I want to explore some of the justifications offered for these reforms. During its second reading in the House of Commons, Purnell justified his Welfare Reform Bill 2008–09 on the now familiar grounds that 'support should be matched with responsibility'. Moreover, he claimed that it would 'change' the lives of people who have been trapped on Incapacity Benefit for too long as well as lone parents who would be in work if they only knew about the jobs available to them. It would also help to deter more people from committing benefit fraud.[27]

It is open to conjecture whether or not the reforms could have the desired effect in the context of rising unemployment and a climate of economic desperation. Nevertheless, it is worth noting that some of the more philosophical justifications for the government's reforms have come from Ed Miliband, a close confidant of Gordon Brown. Traditionally the benches of the House of Commons and the ranks of the civil service have been well represented by graduates from Oxford University. Miliband is a prime example, having read Philosophy, Politics and Economics at Corpus Christi. In his contribution to a new collection of essays on Third Way politics he makes clear his knowledge of recent trends in political philosophy when he argues for a reduction of material inequalities on multiple grounds: that inequalities are often the result of accidents of brute luck; that inequalities undermine social solidarity; and that inequalities reduce the self-respect of the least advantaged. Yet Miliband also acknowledges the objection that it would perpetuate another form of unfairness to force hard-working taxpayers to support people who received benefits without doing or giving anything in return. As he puts it: 'A welfare system that demands appropriate responsibilities is perfectly compatible with egalitarianism.'[28]

Even the government's controversial Work Capability Assessment can be supported by recent egalitarian political philosophy. As discussed in Chapter 3, Elizabeth Anderson is critical of luck egalitarians whom, she argues, put too much emphasis on equality of opportunity, ignoring equality of outcome. According to Anderson, true equality – or 'democratic equality' – requires that *everybody* should have access to the basic capabilities required to evade oppressive or exploitative human relationships and to lead normal lives as respected members of society. Nevertheless, she also insists that 'For those suspected of abusing the worker's disability system, some determination must . . . be made of whether they are actually capable of holding down a job and just malingering, or truly disabled or otherwise effectively unemployable.'[29]

HEALTHCARE REFORM

The NHS is another key battleground for political parties in Britain. At present all legal residents are entitled to health services within the NHS, which are free at the point of delivery and not conditional on having previously made tax contributions. (Private medical insurance remains the preserve of people on higher incomes with unofficial figures suggesting that only around 12.5 per cent of the population have private health insurance.) Even though both of the main political parties in Britain are convinced of the need to radically shake up the NHS, in part by increasing the amount of personal responsibility among patients, concrete proposals have been fraught with difficulty.

In the years running up to the general election in May 2005 the Conservatives championed 'patients' passports', a proposal to give patients the right to opt out of the NHS by receiving up to 60 per cent of the cost of their NHS operation in 'cash back' if they choose to go private. Using the terminology introduced in Chapter 2, this is an example of personal responsibility as autonomy. However, in his first major policy speech after becoming leader of the Conservative Party Cameron dropped the patients' passport policy.[30] The idea of permitting the wealthy to opt out of the NHS taking money with them seemed a regressive policy, allowing the rich to get a better standard of treatment while leaving less money in the pot for everyone else. Where two individuals have the same diagnosed illness, why should one receive better treatment than the other simply because he is wealthier? Here we have a case of equality versus autonomy – advantage equality.

For its part, the Labour government has been wrestling with the issue of 'top-ups', a scheme whereby people are able to purchase for themselves life-saving drugs deemed not cost-effective by their local NHS trusts while remaining as NHS patients and being treated in NHS hospitals by NHS doctors. The government wished to avoid a situation in which patients in the same NHS hospitals received different levels of treatment and so had initially banned top-up payments. But responding to widespread public dismay about the ban, in November 2008 the Health Secretary Alan Johnson was forced to make a U-turn and to allow these payments.[31] If a cancer patient wishes to top up her NHS treatment with a drug which could extend her life without actually making other patients in the NHS worse off, how could the government reasonably object? This seems to be a case of equality versus autonomy – advantage autonomy.

A different set of battles are being fought in the US. Around 84 per cent of American citizens have health insurance either through their employer (60 per cent), private insurance policies (9 per cent), or provided by state and federal government funded programmes (27 per cent) such as Medicaid which provides basic health insurance coverage to the unemployed and the disabled or Medicare which is available to the elderly. This leaves 47 million people without health insurance cover (16 per cent) including students and working families who are on low incomes and not entitled to Medicaid or Medicare. While the US devotes 16 per cent of GDP to health spending, it has relatively poor health as a nation and this is partly due to the lack of universal coverage.[32] Not surprisingly, then, the question of health insurance reform played a significant part in the 2008 US presidential election campaign. Obama promised to bring about comprehensive healthcare by putting pressure on insurance companies not to cherry-pick clients, by giving employers financial credits for their employer-based schemes, by giving poor, uninsured Americans the chance to buy into a federal insurance scheme hitherto only available to government employees and by injecting more money into preventive care. His presidential opponent, John McCain, proposed instead to reduce administrative costs, to give strong incentives to employers to transfer the primary responsibility for purchasing health insurance to employees and to give every American family a $5,000 refundable tax credit to spend on any health insurance plan they wished.[33]

One obvious difference here is that Obama's plan was about establishing ways for people to take responsibility as part of occupational or state schemes, whereas McCain's plan was much more about people taking responsibility as individuals or families. Another interesting difference was that Obama's plan pushed prevention as a way of controlling spending in a way that McCain's did not. Apparently Obama's campaign team did not take seriously – or did not wish to appear to be taking seriously – empirical research in the US showing that in many instances putting more money into preventive healthcare isn't actually cheaper in the end. Multiple studies have shown that preventive measures such as offering mammograms to all women above a certain age or prescribing drugs to everyone with high cholesterol do not save money because they target very large numbers of 'at risk' people, which invariably includes many more individuals than would ever have actually become sick.[34]

Gordon Brown has also made healthcare reform a priority. In January 2008 he stated two main aims. First, 'The NHS of the future will do more than just treat patients who are ill – it will be an NHS offering prevention as well.' This means that 'over time, everyone in England will have access to the right preventative health check-up.' Second, 'The NHS of the future will be more than a universal service – it will be a personal service too. It will not be the NHS of the passive patient – the NHS of the future will be one of patient power, patients engaged and taking greater control over their own health and their healthcare too.' This new 'active role' implies not merely the right to choose one's own hospital but also a personal responsibility to give treatment its best chance of working.[35] Back in July 2007 Brown commissioned Lord Darzi to write a report on how best to meet the challenges of healthcare over the coming decades. The brief included the drawing up of an NHS constitution for England establishing the core principles and values of the NHS and setting out patients' rights and responsibilities. The draft NHS constitution is now in the public domain and contains a long list of patient responsibilities including:

> You should recognise that you can make a significant contribution to your own, and your family's, good health, and take some personal responsibility for it.
> You should keep appointments.

> You should follow the course of treatment which you have agreed with your clinician.[36]

David Cameron and the Conservatives have now also jumped on board the preventive health bandwagon. In August 2008 Cameron asked David Lewis, the chairman of Unilever UK, to chair a working group of business representatives, voluntary groups and experts to work out the finer details of a pact between the government and private business on issues relating to people's health. Initial proposals for dealing with the 'obesity time-bomb' included industry-led reductions on food portion sizes, positive attempts by food companies and the government to promote better diets, and financial incentives for small and medium-sized companies to improve the health of their employees through health and fitness clubs.[37]

A political philosopher reflecting on these initiatives is left with a number of questions. My own is this: what is the moral justification for this emphasis on preventive responsibility, especially when preventive medicine may not actually be cheaper in the long run? The justification appears to have two main parts. On the one hand, there is an obvious paternalistic edge to these reforms. Politicians will argue that it is one of the central functions of the state to pre- serve public health. Whatever else one thinks about what it means to lead a flourishing life, few people would say that being unfit and unhealthy is compatible with doing well. Rather than trying to impose an outright ban on junk food, the government should do what it can to increase information and work with the food indus- try to encourage personal responsibility. This, politicians say, is not infantilising members of the public but imploring them to be healthier, which is a rational preference. On the other hand, there is an appeal to fairness as reciprocity lurking here. Although few British politicians feel able to challenge the core principle of 'free at the point of delivery', there is a move to ask patients to do their bit by taking responsibility for their own health. This is a matter of fairness to other patients and taxpayers.

But now there is a second question. Given the emphasis on individuals acting more responsibly in relation to their own health as well as their own healthcare, what should be the consequences for those individuals who fail to live up to their new responsibilities? In other words, a list of patient responsibilities is one way of transferring responsibility to the individual, but the question is whether having given these responsibilities to patients the government is now rightfully in a position to say that the consequences of failing to live up to those responsibilities are appropriately borne by the patient. Under the present system, doctors and NHS trusts are not permitted to discriminate between patients on the basis of their irresponsibility. Nevertheless, is this sort of discrimination now on the horizon and, if so, would it be justified?

I shall return to the issue of health responsibilities in Chapter 7, but for now I want to focus on the more general idea of balancing rights and responsibilities.

RIGHTS AND RESPONSIBILITIES

The idea of balancing rights and responsibilities has been central to New Labour's reforms over the past ten years or so and now figures heavily in the Conservative Party's plans for the future. Tony Blair was a huge admirer of the ideas of Anthony Giddens, Emeritus Professor at the London School of Economics. Giddens identified 'No rights without responsibilities' as one of the core principles of the Third Way. Writing in the *Guardian* in 2006, Blair similarly declared that 'we must balance rights with responsibilities.' 'On welfare reform we need to go further with the principle of new entitlements matched by higher expectations.'[38] If New Labour stole the clothes of the political right by emphasising rights and responsibilities, Cameron has worked hard to reclaim the idea for the Conservatives. The idea of formally linking responsibilities with the rights of citizens has been a notable theme of his leadership. Speaking at the launch of the Young Adult Trust charity in October 2006, for example, he proposed that young people should be given their adult rights as a reward for completing a modern day national service scheme.[39]

How exactly are these rights and responsibilities to be articulated? David Cameron and Gordon Brown have both advocated the idea of establishing a Bill of Rights and Responsibilities for the British people. Cameron's proposal came in June 2006 during a period in which he was attempting to consolidate his power and unite the Party around his leadership. He argued that 'a modern British bill of rights needs to define the core values which give us our identity as a free nation' and to 'spell out the fundamental duties and responsibilities of people living in this country'.[40] Brown made his move during his leadership campaign speech in May 2007 when he declared: 'We need a constitution that is clear about the rights and responsibilities of being a citizen in Britain today.'[41] While Cameron envisaged a panel of experts to draft the new Bill of Rights and Responsibilities, Brown sought to confirm his democratic credentials by asking Michael Wills, the newly appointed Minister of State for the Ministry of Justice, to embark on a large public consultation exercise on a statement of British values culminating in a Citizens' Summit with 1,000 people deliberating on these values.

A cynic might say that the only reason why politicians support a Bill of Rights and Responsibilities for Britain is because they want to stop British citizens from claiming their human rights either through the Human Rights Act 1998 which incorporated into UK law the 1950 European Convention on Human Rights or by appealing directly to the European Court of Human Rights in Strasbourg. A more plausible explanation is that politicians are worried that ordinary people are vastly more aware of their rights nowadays and have lost sight of their responsibilities. A Bill of Rights and Responsibilities would make it clearer that the right to healthcare, for example, comes with certain responsibilities, such as the responsibility to follow doctor's orders after an operation. This will then enable politicians to better manage the funding of care services. Many of the responsibilities discussed in this debate are best described as role responsibilities, where the relevant role is that of citizen.

Now, in 2007 the Labour government commissioned a House of Commons Joint Committee on Human Rights to consider the merits of a Bill of Rights for Britain including the issue of whether or not the Bill should refer to responsibilities. In addition to the constitutional issue of whether or not Britain could adopt its own Bill of Rights and remain a signatory to the European Convention on Human Rights, several concerns came to light. One concern was that a Bill of Rights and Responsibilities might seem to conditionalise rights. According to a number of witnesses to the Committee, the proposition that rights must be earned or are in the gift of the government depending on the performance of one's responsibilities flies in the face of the fundamental idea of human rights as universal and inalienable. For example, to what extent are health responsibilities compatible with the idea of a human right to healthcare? A second concern relates to the fact that the intended purpose of the Bill of Rights and Responsibilities was not necessarily to make responsibilities enforceable in law but to emphasise their importance in a fair society. In this way responsibilities are supposed to be more symbol than judicial entities. But if this is the case then it is open to question whether or not a Bill of Rights and Responsibilities is the appropriate vehicle. For this reason the Committee recommended that a Bill of Rights should not include a set of enforceable responsibilities.[42]

My own concerns are as follows. First, politicians talk of balancing rights and responsibilities. This implies that the two things can be measured on the same set of scales, where fairness has something to do with equal amounts of each. But why assume that rights and responsibilities are commensurable in this way? And why equal amounts?

My second concern is with the logical relationship between rights and responsibilities. Consider the relationship between legal rights and legal duties. Some philosophers argue that legal rights are connected to legal duties in the following way. To say that person A has a right is to say that A has a right against person B to do or not do X. Person A can be said to have a right against person B *only if* person B has a corresponding duty to honour A's right. If B has no such duty, then A has no such right. So, for example, someone's right to the exclusive use of his own garden entails a correlative duty on the part of other people not to trespass. Furthermore, in many legal systems around the world the right to use one's own property is limited in the following way. Property holders have a responsibility not to interfere with their neighbours' rights to use and enjoy their property, such as by polluting their neighbour's garden with thick black smoke, and must accept responsibility for any pollution that they do cause.[43]

What, then, is the connection between the kinds of social rights and responsibilities that politicians are interested in? Perhaps the idea is that having a right to unemployment benefits and public healthcare implies – if not logically entails – a corresponding responsibility to do one's bit to keep the system going. Unless a large proportion of citizens assume responsibility by working for a living, paying their taxes and avoiding ill-health, tax revenues will fall through the floor, the pressure on the social system will be too great and the state will be unable to fulfil citizens' rights to unemployment benefits and public healthcare. In that sense having access to the objects of social rights depends on most people performing their responsibilities. This is a practical connection if not a conceptual connection.

However, even this practical argument proceeds too quickly: for it is perfectly possible for *some* citizens to enjoy these rights without doing their bit towards the creation of the social good. That is, it is quite possible for some citizens to enjoy their rights without fulfilling their responsibilities. The upshot is that we need an argument to show why it is morally fitting for *all* citizens to fulfil their responsibilities.

It seems to me that Labour's main justification for connecting responsibilities with rights rests not on the idea of gratitude to the state for the gift of rights but on the different notion of fair play between members of society. According to this view, when citizens contribute their taxes to the common pool – from which money is drawn to aid those suffering from various hardships and disadvantages – it creates a duty of fair play (or fair reciprocity) on recipients of aid to do their bit. Those who receive assistance from the common pool should recognise that they have a responsibility either to find work and pay their taxes or to contribute to society in some other way such as through voluntary work. Brown summed up this idea in 2000:

> Some say Britain is home to a selfish culture, that today British people place far less value on personal and social responsibility as a moral good, less importance on what we owe others as a matter of moral obligation and more weight on personal self gratification and individual advancement at the expense of duty to others. Indeed some write of a middle England whose comforts make it forget a poor Britain of places and peoples left behind. I believe that the opposite is true: that one of our great British qualities has always been – and is today – our strong sense of personal and civic responsibility and reciprocity – an understanding that those who benefit from citizenship have also an obligation to give something back in return. This is what defines us at our best.[44]

The basic contention is that *if* people are willing to regard society as a system of fair cooperation over the course of their lives, then it is appropriate for them to accept a fair balance of rights and responsibilities as one of the touchstones of that society. But then this raises the following obvious question: why should citizens recognise this as a system of fair cooperation in the first place? Why shouldn't they see this as an elaborate farce? Why should a taxpayer continue to contribute if he sincerely believes that he gets nothing of comparable (let alone equal) value in return? Why should the welfare recipient bother to look for more productive ways to contribute to society, such as by earning a living and paying taxes, if he or she can get away with not doing so?

One response to this challenge is to insist that all individuals born within well-ordered democratic states have a natural duty to uphold and support the system of fair cooperation. But maybe this amounts to banging one's fist on the table and declaring 'Why do you have the responsibility to participate in this system? Well, you just do!' So what else can we say? One thought might be that the basis on which the government can reasonably expect reciprocal cooperation by taxpayers and welfare recipients is shared values or culture. The problem with this argument, however, is that it seems ill-suited to the kind of multicultural societies in which we find ourselves, where there is a reasonable plurality of values and cultures. The point is certainly not lost on the prominent Conservative politician David ('two brains') Willetts:

> The basis on which you can extract large sums of money in tax and pay it out in benefits is that most people think the recipients are people like themselves facing difficulties that they themselves could face. If values become more diverse, if lifestyles become more differentiated, then it becomes more difficult to sustain the legitimacy of a universal risk pooling welfare state. People ask: why should I pay for them when they are doing things that I wouldn't do? This is America versus Sweden. You can have a Swedish welfare state provided that you are a homogeneous society with intensely shared values. In the United States you have a very diverse, individualistic society where people feel fewer obligations to fellow citizens. Progressives want diversity, but they thereby undermine part of the moral consensus on which a large welfare state rests.[45]

Some people look to national identity as the tie that could bind people together. Few academics have done more to articulate and give reasonable expression to this line of thought than David Miller, Professor of Political Theory at Nuffield College, Oxford University. He argues that it is unwise to capitulate to every demand that is put forward under the heading of 'multiculturalism' given that this often comes at the expense of national solidarity and the withering of the welfare state.[46] Many politicians agree with Miller that the appropriate basis on which citizens can be asked to make mutual sacrifices is some form of national citizenship. Indeed, it is plausible to interpret New Labour's stance on rights and responsibilities as part of a broader ambition to reinvigorate the role of citizenship in British society. During his speech to the Labour Party conference in September 2006, for example, Brown spoke of the need to forge a shared national purpose 'that can unify us all'. He added: 'we the British people must be far more explicit about the common ground on which we stand, the shared values which bring us together, the habits of citizenship around which we can and must unite'.[47]

But what are these shared values? It is surely a sign of the difficulty of pinning down such things that Brown's description of 'the enduring British values' has undergone many revisions over a relatively short space of time. In January 2006 he declared that 'in addition to our qualities of creativity, inventiveness, enterprise and our internationalism, our central beliefs are a commitment to – liberty for all, responsibility by all and fairness to all'.[48] By the time of the Labour Party conference in September 2006 the shared values were identified as 'fair play, respect, a decent chance in life' and 'the truth, that as individual citizens of Britain we must act upon the responsibilities we owe to each other as well as our rights'.[49] Brown's speeches on British citizenship merge the ideal of personal responsibility with the goal of civic renewal, so that personal responsibility includes both taking responsibility for one's own livelihood and acting as a responsible citizen. The latter means doing one's bit in the public domain including participating in public decisions such as those about the balance of rights and responsibilities in society.

It is not certain how well defined any of these values are or whether they could offer practical guidance to policymakers in determining what we owe to each other. But what is most interesting about Brown's descriptions is that they bring us back full circle to the idea of rights and responsibilities with which we started. So the question we need to ask ourselves is this: What is to stop the welfare state from collapsing like a deck of cards once individuals realise that they have no independent reason to accept the set of rights and responsibilities handed down to them by government? That they share a deep understanding, common purpose and strong national identity may provide the answer in some political communities. But what about countries like Britain which is more fractured and heterogeneous? Today there is a white majority in England that feels under threat from restless nationalist groups in Scotland, Wales and Northern Ireland as well as from immigrant populations, isolationist religious groups, migrant workers, asylum seekers and assorted resident non-citizens. Arguably this makes the chances of securing genuine and heartfelt loyalty to a single national consciousness and common way of life vanishingly small.

No doubt there is much to be said for reviving a sense of national identity and pride.[50] But there are also dangers. One is that focusing too heavily on nation-based conceptions of citizenship might lead to a regime of nationality tests which excludes vulnerable immigrant groups from access to basic social services such as health, education and housing. This is personal responsibility by default and it is open to question. Another danger is that a policy of reinvigorating national identity might prove too successful. If welfare rights and responsibilities are tied to national belonging, what is to stop this from resulting in a splintering of social services? We already have NHS Scotland for the Scottish. Should the government set up a dedicated NHS for British Pakistanis living in the north of England to reflect their mixed national identity? Attaching different rights and responsibilities to the members of different national groups could make things easier in some ways. Yet breaking up the NHS is also likely to have implications for efficiency, not least in terms of economies of scale. What is more, it may have unforeseen and deleterious consequences for individuals in certain national groups. Some women and disabled people may find themselves living within a national group that provides them with limited personal responsibility for making judgements about their own health and welfare. Others may find that they are torn between multiple national identities, forever having to juggle conflicting sets of rights and responsibilities.[51]

Partly because of these problems, some politicians and political think tanks endorse a democratic conception of citizenship, in which all citizens are expected to play an active role in making decisions on social policy and various other areas of government.[52] What would it take to make people happy – if that is the right word – for the government to extract large sums of money in tax and pay it out in benefits to people they do not know personally and who are potentially not like them? Answer: by increasing the amount of public engagement in the relevant social policy decisions. Of course, the practical difficulty remains how to deliver this public engagement on a grand scale and in ways that unite rather than divide people.

I shall take up this question again in Chapter 8, but for now I want to return to the proposal of a new Bill of Rights and Responsibilities in Britain.

Although in the end the Joint Committee on Human Rights recommended not incorporating a list of responsibilities within a Bill of Rights, they did suggest that the language of responsibilities could play a role in its Preamble.[53] I have some sympathy with this compromise suggestion, but I also think that there is another measure that could be taken that falls between the extremes of either including or excluding a list of responsibilities within the Bill of Rights. My slightly different proposal is for a right to personal responsibility to be included as one of the social and economic rights to be stated in the Bill. This right may not be able to replace all of the specific responsibilities that the government wished to include, but it does make an important point. If the government is really serious about people taking greater personal responsibility for the success or failure of their own lives, then it should first establish a right to exercise such responsibility. No doubt there could be many different formulations, but while we wait for the Citizens' Summit to deliver its recommendations, here is one that strikes me as worthy of consideration.

The Right to Personal Responsibility

Everyone has a right to personal responsibility. No one shall be deprived of the right to personal responsibility save in the promotion and protection of the capacity for personal responsibility.

Everyone has the right to exercise his or her capacity for personal responsibility including the right to gain access to a decent standard of living through the exercise of his capacity for personal responsibility.

The state has a responsibility to ensure that people can exercise their capacity for personal responsibility and shall not be regarded as contravening the right to personal responsibility when it works to provide education, social security and healthcare for those who lack the capacity for personal responsibility.

Perhaps this suggestion will seem provocative or absurd to those people who are concerned by too much talk of rights and not enough talk of responsibilities. But the right to personal responsibility has two distinctive implications. The first is that it builds into the Bill of Rights a firm commitment on the part of the state to promote personal responsibility, with everything that this implies about the value and importance of such responsibilities. The second implication of recognising the right to personal responsibility is that in theory someone could suffer an injustice merely by lacking the opportunity to look after him or herself in some suitable way, such as through paid employment. In so far as the state has an obligation to promote the right to personal responsibility it would have an obligation to provide the opportunities required to exercise that right.

However, this proposal leaves the question of personal responsibilities hanging. How can the state make clear the particular responsibilities of individuals? A Bill of Responsibilities is by its nature rigid and incomplete. It is a statement of responsibilities of its moment and necessarily abstract in order to give it any hope of applying across contexts and time. So how else can the state resolve the question of personal responsibilities? One way is to establish a democratic procedure or set of democratic institutions for working out personal responsibilities in different areas of public policy. That is, to create an appropriate public political procedure by which responsibilities can be formulated democratically, so that responsibilities are complete, dynamic and by the people. At any given time the responsibilities should give expression to the idea of fair reciprocity in society. Nevertheless, the democratic authority of these responsibilities is reposed in the fairness of the procedures that create them rather than in a rigid list and its juridical interpretation. Having set out a new right to personal responsibility in this chapter, in Chapter 8 I consider how this right might be implemented democratically through the use of citizens' juries.

ON THE RESPONSIBILITIES OF POLITICIANS

At the Conservative Party conference in October 2008 Cameron made the following pledge on responsibility. 'Every big decision; every big judgement I make: I ask myself some simple questions. Does this encourage responsibility and discourage irresponsibility?'[54] I agree that this is one of the big questions that politicians should ask. But it seems to me that they should also ask another question: how can we as politicians be more responsible when it comes to developing social policies?

For one thing, politicians should be more responsible about when and how they demand responsibility from ordinary people. Politicians are fond of saying that the state can't do it all. As Cameron puts it, 'In the end, the best regulation is self-regulation, not state regulation.'[55] This is no doubt true in many cases. But politicians don't always start out with reasonable expectations about what can be done by the individuals concerned. One point worth making here is that once individuals have got themselves into difficulty it is by no means always possible for them to get themselves out of difficulty. Suppose we say to the person with a heroin addiction that the best regulation is self-regulation. This may be on a par with saying to someone stuck in quicksand that since he stupidly ignored the warning signs it is his responsibility to get himself out. The point is that once he is stuck in the sand he can't do much to save himself and the more he kicks the worse it can get. It is society that possesses the rope that will stop him sinking further, and it can choose to throw that lifeline or not. Of course, some responsibility for seeking or accepting help must also reside with the problem user himself. Yet a common characteristic of what it means to be a problem user can be to lack the wherewithal to do something about it alone.

In some instances politicians will act in response to the general advice of policy experts, only to pursue flawed policies. For example, governments are told that a better system of social welfare can be one that is cruder in the distinctions it draws than the actual problems it is designed to tackle. One reason is public confusion about what benefits are available. This can cause too little take up. However, making the benefits system too simple can cause the opposite problem of too much take up. Tax credits provide one illustration. Launched by Brown in 2003 the tax credit system aimed to help around six million families and 600,000 workers on low incomes. Tax credits are sums of money paid by the government directly into people's bank accounts. Tax credits have helped a lot of people out of extreme poverty, which itself can be a major barrier to personal responsibility. But the House of Commons Committee of Public Accounts has also reported that the government overpaid £6 billion in the first three years of the scheme because of error and fraud.[56] It is no doubt true that sometimes authorities may have to give a little more to people than they may be strictly entitled to, and to others a little less, in order to achieve a good result all things considered. But this depends on there being good results to achieve. It is difficult to see the advantages of £6 billion given over to error and fraud.

Sometimes social policies fail because they go against the grain of human nature or because they are hopelessly vulnerable to the frailties and vices of ordinary people. So understanding why individuals don't exercise personal responsibility is something that politicians need to work on. Some appear to think that the individuals concerned must be lacking in moral fibre. Others point out that the system makes it in people's self-interest to be dependent on the state. If unemployment benefits were less generous and if rules on bankruptcy were more severe, fewer people would rely on the state to give them income and fewer would allow themselves to get into personal debt. Others point out that there is a hard-core of individuals who will remain idle or get into debt regardless of whether the government's response is draconian or not. So they blame families, teachers and sub-cultures for failing to inculcate the appropriate values. Still others insist that the biggest single cause of a lack of personal responsibility today is the absence of equality of opportunity for all. If people do not think they have a fair chance, they will not be motivated to try. In so far as the success or failure of social policies depends on the accuracy of these explanations, politicians would do well to commission more social research to find out.

Faced with seemingly intractable social problems there is also a tendency among politicians to resort to saying things like, 'What we need is a revolution in social attitudes and behaviour.' Although they sometimes admit that their proposals are utopian, in the sense of requiring a different social ethos, politicians also insist that their proposals are not hopelessly utopian provided that new attitudes and behaviour could be taught and internalised by large numbers of people over time. In other words, the politician will be effectively saying that the problem is not that he has the wrong solution for society but that we currently have the wrong kind of society for the right solution. One fairly obvious drawback with this way of thinking, however, is that it ignores the fact – or has a tendency to ignore the fact – that making changes to the social ethos imposes different kinds of costs. Some costs can be measured simply in financial terms, such as paying for the necessary changes in education. But the loss of existing values and culture is itself a cost and it may be difficult to measure that cost against what the politician hopes to gain.

Politicians are also guilty of mimicking media sensationalism about social problems. Consider recent advertising campaigns used by the government to tackle the problem of welfare fraud, which according to some estimates costs more than £1 billion a year. The television and poster campaigns, make the point that benefit fraud is theft and therefore on a par with other acquisitive crime. They also include an appeal to ordinary members of the public to report suspected benefits cheats, akin to neighbourhood watch schemes. But these ads attract a number of criticisms. One is that the advertising campaigns actually increased the numbers of fraudulent claims as people realised how easy it must be to do it.[57] A second is that these campaigns are in danger of creating a vicious circle in which governments try to respond to public perceptions about high levels of welfare fraud and in so doing further enhance those perceptions which in turn creates more pressure on government to get even tougher.

I wish to make two final points about the responsibilities of politicians. The first relates to opposition politicians. Savings and pensions is one area where the state can do much to promote personal responsibility. It can, for example, do what Cameron has recently proposed, which is to reduce taxes paid on savings interest to encourage individuals to make preparations for a rainy day. But opposition politicians – no less than those in government – have a responsibility to make promises which they can afford to keep. It is irresponsible to make promises of tax cuts without having the proper funding; it is bitterly ironic to make such promises in relation to promoting personal responsibility.[58]

My second point relates to those in power. It is a truism not emphasised enough that when a government assumes the task of promoting a set of values a failure to follow through on that endeavour can have a more deleterious impact on people's lives than if it had done nothing. Take the case of company pensions. During the late 1980s and early 1990s millions of employees were advised to leave their company pension schemes. The Conservative government promoted private pensions in the name of freedom and prosperity. Despite this, private pensions ended up being bad value for money for thousands of people. Blair's Labour government blamed the Tories and soon persuaded thousands of people to take responsibility for their future by once again paying into company pension schemes, with contributions from the state. In time some of these companies went bankrupt with the collapse of the pension schemes and the loss of people's retirement savings. Initially the government tried to claim that since these weren't actually state pensions it had no obligation to bail people out. But since 2006 it has come under increasing pressure from trade unions, MPs and the House of Lords to significantly increase the amount of compensation given to the victims. It is likely that the government will have to accept the principle that when individuals are encouraged by the government to join or remain in company pension schemes, it has a responsibility to underwrite the losses. Doing so sends out a clear signal to society: the government cares about personal responsibility and it will act consistently and with determination to ensure that individuals who are willing to assume personal responsibility are protected.

The moral of this story is that if governments are going to accuse ordinary citizens of not showing enough personal responsibility for the success or failure of their own lives, they must expect to be judged by similar standards. Politicians tend to be very future-oriented creatures, forever planning the next policy intervention and dreaming up new proposals that might 'play well' with the electorate. This is not entirely their fault, of course, for they must operate under a system of periodic elections. Nevertheless, there is an inclination in politics to equate 'the good' with change.

But arguably politicians ought to show greater self-discipline by not speeding from one policy initiative to the next and by faithfully carrying out initiatives once started. There is also a need for greater 'joined up' government. What does that mean? It means that members of the Cabinet should work together to promote a given set of principles and values consistently rather than promoting a value with one policy only for that value to be undermined by policies in another government department. Needless to say, politicians should also act more responsibly when it comes to living within their means and not making claims on expenses that are unreasonable, greedy and in some instances fraudulent. If politicians would like individuals to start behaving more responsibly, then perhaps they should set an example by behaving more responsibly in these important respects.

6   What Do Ordinary People Think?

There are people who are single parents, who don't work, who get everything in terms of benefits thrown at them. It should be the other way round. I'm willing to go out there to work to provide for my kids. I think if you are capable of working you should work.

Clare Mawer, 34, from Coventry

The stereotype of single parents is young girls who get pregnant to get a council house but other people have different circumstances and a system should be there to help people.

Kyla Manners, 45, from Brighton

Having set out some prominent lines of philosophical and political thinking on the nature and importance of personal responsibility, this chapter looks at what ordinary people think on the subject. As noted in Chapter 1, some contemporary philosophers, although not all, believe that the task of understanding political concepts and weighing their relative importance may be helped rather than hindered by sifting through empirical research about what ordinary people think. But how, more precisely, can this sort of evidence be useful? What is the point of looking at opinion surveys? What, if anything, do these opinions reveal about personal responsibility? And what is the best method of gathering these opinions? I begin with a deceptively simple question.

WHY ASK?

There is more than one rationale for philosophers taking an interest in public opinion surveys. One starts from the limits of philosophical imagination. Although philosophers are adept at identifying and clarifying principles of morality, they can't be expected to dream up every idea. Opinion surveys may provide invaluable insights into principles not yet on the philosopher's radar. Philosophers are also ingenious when it comes to working out the relative importance of different parts of the moral system. Some philosophers argue that rights are best understood as trumps over other social goods, for example. But it is not always clear-cut when one principle or value should take priority over another, and looking at opinion surveys may provide useful clues.

Be that as it may, what is the status of this evidence? Some philosophers – call them intuitionists – believe that certain moral truths are self-evident, meaning we can know them to be true without giving further justifications for them. These truths are writ large, so to speak, in the nature of things and discoverable through our faculty of moral intuition. The form of intuitionism I have in mind also comes with ontological baggage. It says that the things human beings have moral intuitions about are not physical but metaphysical. We may not be able to touch justice and goodness, but they are a part of the fabric of the universe nevertheless, just as much as numbers are. Intuitionists are not committed to making swift transitions from intuitions about right and wrong to decisions about social policy. On the contrary, they believe that we must seek out those intuitions about which we feel most confident, perhaps intuitions that are shared by a great many other people. Public opinion surveys do not make ethical propositions true or false. What makes ethical propositions true or false is the realm of entities, qualities or relations to which they correspond or fail to correspond. Nevertheless, this evidence may constitute reasons to feel more secure in paying particular attention to certain intuitions.

Other philosophers, by contrast – call them constructivists – think that it is unnecessary to posit the existence of a special realm of metaphysical entities in order to talk meaningfully about justice and goodness. Constructivists believe instead that what gives meaning to the claims people make about right and wrong is the fact that a large number of us are willing to make them and in similar ways. This sort of philosopher might look upon evidence from opinion surveys not so much as reasons to feel more secure about our intuitions but as social facts that need to be explained or accounted for. The aim of the theory is to reflect on this data alongside our other ordinary beliefs and practices and to try to construct the best or most coherent system of thought possible. That is, we try to construct the best theory out of what people ordinarily think.

Both of these methodologies have their strengths and weaknesses. Some people find intuitionism rather strange. Why should we believe that the universe contains things which by their very nature provide us with reasons for action and that guide action in specific ways? What is this human faculty which allows us to detect moral facts? Isn't it arrogant to think that intuitions are anything more than personal preferences? And if moral truths are self-evident, how come even the most learned philosophers disagree about them? On the other hand, some people believe that the weakness of constructivism is its tendency to favour the status quo. If part of the point of having a theory of justice is to provide impetus for change in society, to make things more just, surely this point is lost if we construct a theory of justice from what most people already think and do. These are deep disagreements, but not unexpected. Part of what makes political philosophy a philosophy and not a science is that there is such disagreement about how to do it. Two of the greatest political philosophers of the second half of the twentieth century, Rawls and Nozick, were working concurrently at Harvard University yet reached very different conclusions not only about the right principles of justice for the society in which they both lived, but also about how to do political philosophy. Rawls was a constructivist, liberal egalitarian; Nozick an intuitionist, libertarian.

I do not intend to settle this dispute here. Instead I wish to make the different point that neither of these methodologies entails that we should be slavish to public opinions. An intuitionist need not suppose that moral truths are self-evident to everyone all of the time. So even if an opinion survey or series of opinion surveys revealed a widespread public attitude that all unemployed people are lazy and don't deserve any social support whatsoever, the intuitionist is not required to accept this as an intuition of the appropriate sort. The opinion expressed might be masking a range of factual errors, biases or prejudices. It may even be that the people surveyed lack a properly developed moral faculty. For his part, the constructivist can say that the best theory is one that casts out certain popular opinions if they have no place within the best overall system of thought.

Even if evidence from opinion surveys should be taken with a pinch of salt as regards to 'the truth', however, a different rationale lends a sort of pragmatic credence to popular opinion. Because any proposed social policy must ultimately command a good deal of compliance from the public if it is going to be successful, we need a way of gauging possible levels of compliance when drawing up a list of potential policies. In this vein, evidence from opinion surveys might be viewed as grounds for making predictions about whether a given policy will be accepted or, in contrast to this, might cause riots on the streets. Reflecting on this evidence could therefore enable political philosophers and policymakers alike to satisfy what Rawls called 'the strains of commitment': it is reasonable to favour principles of political morality that will command widespread compliance among the public due to the fact that all things considered its demands will not be intolerable for most people. If public opinion can be used to make passably accurate predictions about public compliance, we have a *prima facie* reason to judge what should be done politically by looking more closely at such opinion.

Nevertheless, we should not preclude the possibility that what social justice really demands is a radical change to what people currently think. Indeed, we must not forget the role that governments play in forming public opinions. If people hold certain opinions about a particular policy issue, this might be because the government has done a good job in getting its message into the public arena. Perhaps ordinary people would be similarly compelled by a different set of answers if they heard more about them. Nevertheless, public opinion surveys may yet provide invaluable markers for where the public stands at the current moment and what philosophers might need to do in terms of changing minds. If, for example, it is demonstrated that public support for greater personal responsibility is relatively low, then one of the most useful functions that public opinion surveys could fulfil is in making clear how much work needs to be done in terms of re-educating the public. The philosopher can then assist policymakers in advancing particular policy issues by offering reasons as to why personal responsibility is a right or good thing.

Having outlined some possible rationales for consulting evidence from public opinion surveys, I now turn to explore what ordinary people think about personal responsibility. I begin with attitudes to welfare claimants.

ATTITUDES TO WELFARE CLAIMANTS

Although there has been a long tradition of social welfare in Britain – provided through trade unions, professional associations, friendly societies and workers' cooperatives – the Poor Laws of England represented the first major attempt to improve the living conditions and quality of life of the poor. Nevertheless, the 1601 Poor Relief Act made a distinction between the 'deserving poor', such as able-bodied workers receiving 'the parish loaf' and the sick, the elderly and orphans receiving 'indoor relief' within parish workhouses, and the 'undeserving poor', which meant 'sturdy beggars' who roamed the highways and byways. The latter could expect to be whipped and either returned to their place of birth or sent to Houses of Correction where they could be put to work. According to some social scientists, something akin to the distinction between 'the deserving' and 'the undeserving' poor lives on in people's attitudes today.[1]

However, the creation of the welfare state in Britain has engendered a more complex set of public attitudes to welfare claimants. After the Second World War the population accepted state intervention as the right way to tackle large social problems. In 1941 the Liberal–Conservative coalition government commissioned William Beveridge to write a report exploring the future provision of social welfare in Britain. The 1942 Beveridge Report recommended that the government fight the five 'giant evils' of want, disease, ignorance, squalor and idleness through the creation of a social security system and national health service for all, and by aiming at full employment. Attlee's 1945–51 Labour government set about constructing the welfare state which remains largely intact today. Indeed, the British Social Attitudes Survey, which began in 1983, reveals that there is still a widespread presumption that the state should be responsible for a range of social needs. The 21st Report (published in 2004) found that when asked who should be responsible for the costs of elderly care, for medical treatment when people get sick and for ensuring that people have enough income to live on should they become sick, disabled or unemployed, in each type of case more than 80 per cent of respondents say that the government should be responsible as compared to between 7 and 14 per cent who say that individuals or their families should be responsible. Attitudes are slightly different in relation to pensions, however, as 58 per cent of people think that the government should be responsible for ensuring that people have enough money in retirement as compared to 29 per cent who regard individuals as responsible.[2]

It would be a mistake to conclude from this, however, that the British people are not interested in personal responsibility: for it is

by no means inconsistent to be committed to personal responsibility and to think that it is right for individuals to come together
to take personal responsibility for their own welfare through
collective action. Of course, some people maintain that social
security is antithetical to real personal responsibility, which they
see as a matter of complete independence from government. But
this conception of personal responsibility is not particularly widespread in Britain. Most people think of personal responsibility as a
matter of not taking a 'free ride' on the state as opposed to having
complete independence from the state.

Interestingly, some liberal egalitarians argue that the more
prosperous a society becomes the more concerned it will be
about neutrality between different conceptions of the good
life and the less concerned it will be about free-riding. Andrew
Levine, for example, defends unconditional basic income on the
grounds that the state has a duty to remain neutral between different conceptions of the good life, not merely in the sense of not
regarding one sort of life as intrinsically better than another but
also in terms of subsidising different lifestyles. Liberal neutrality
implies basic income even for persons who wish to surf all day
rather than work for a living.[3]

But this argument is not well supported by social attitudes
in Britain. There is a popular belief that able-bodied adults of
working age have an obligation to work for a living wherever possible or else contribute to society in some other way. A number
of researchers working in this area maintain that most people
are not particularly in favour of redistribution from the rich to
the poor unconditionally. They prefer instead more fine-grained
patterns of redistribution such as giving public money to those
poor people who are unable to work, who make an effort to
find work or who give something back to society, but reducing
public assistance for those who do not fall into these categories.
According to these researchers, public attitudes in Britain display
a general commitment to fairness as reciprocity. Unconditional
basic income violates the demands of fairness as reciprocity

because it detaches access to income from the basic requirement of making an effort to find work or else make some other contribution to society.[4]

Of course, what these attitudes might show is that the British just aren't rich enough yet to be in a position to stop caring about free-riders. But then this leaves unanswered exactly how rich a country must be before it stops caring. Besides, there is something peculiar about the idea that neutrality demands state subsidy for all conceptions of the good. Surely we don't think that the state should be neutral about *every* lifestyle. As Wolff points out, if as a society we refuse to tolerate the lifestyle choices of white collar fraudsters, why should we feel obliged to bankroll the lifestyle choices of beach bums?[5]

At any rate, results from the 20th Report of the British Social Attitudes Survey (published in 2003) show that there was a hardening of public opinion towards welfare benefits between 1987 and 2002. So, for example, in 1987 more respondents disagreed than agreed with the claim 'If welfare benefits weren't so generous people would learn to stand on their own two feet.' By 2002, however, the situation had reversed and more respondents agreed than disagreed.[6] The 24th Report (published in 2008) also reveals a shift in attitudes toward different groups. In 1986, 64 per cent of respondents identified extra spending on retirement pensions as an appropriate first or second priority for social security, and by 2005 this figure had increased to 80 per cent. Analogous support for extra spending on benefits for single parents, however, dropped from 18 per cent in 1986 to 15 per cent in 2005. In the case of extra spending on benefits for unemployed people, the level of support fell dramatically from 33 per cent in 1986 to 7 per cent in 2005.[7]

That there has been a hardening of public opinion toward single parents and unemployed people in recent decades mirrors the welfare reforms pursued by the Tory government during the 1980s and continued by New Labour in the 1990s and 2000s. During this time there has been a steady shift in the state's response to unemployed people, exemplified by a rising tide of interviews, eligibility assessments and work requirements. It is open to conjecture whether the change in public attitudes sparked the change in social policy or whether the change in social policy influenced public attitudes. It is also a matter for speculation how much the present economic downturn will affect these attitudes. But it seems probable, to me at least, that opinions will soften amid the realization that unemployment and redundancy are out of the control of a great many people.

So what do British people think their government should do in order to tackle the perennial problems of unemployment and welfare dependency? Consider the use of sanctions against those claimants who fail to attend interviews or accept reasonable offers of work or training, where 'sanctions' means having benefits stopped for a period of time. Once again, support for sanctions depends on what type of claimant one is talking about. When asked about the use of sanctions against sick or disabled persons who fail to attend interviews to talk about ways of finding work, 41 per cent of respondents say that benefits should not be affected. When the same question is asked about lone parents, however, only 17 per cent say that benefits should not be affected and 38 per cent say benefits should be reduced a little.[8]

Do the above attitudes vary along political party lines? The answer is yes and no. On the one hand, public attitudes toward the welfare state in general do seem to diverge along fairly familiar political dividing lines. There is strong support among traditional Labour voters for the welfare state, where this means generous assistance both for the working man and for the socially excluded. These voters are characteristically opposed to cuts in benefits and regard sanctions as an unwelcome attempt to demonise certain sections of society. They regard some of New Labour's reforms as at best meanness and at worse gross unfairness: reducing the welfare rolls is a ploy to win votes among middle-class taxpayers and it comes at the expense of the poor and the vulnerable. Conservative voters, by contrast, tend to have a less positive perspective on the welfare state. In a 2003 study 67 per cent of Conservative respondents agreed with the statement 'The welfare state makes people nowadays less willing to look after themselves' as compared to just 35 per cent of Labour supporters.[9]

On the other hand, there seems to be hardly any variation across the political spectrum when it comes to the appropriateness of sanctions against particular groups of welfare claimants. For example, asked whether or not benefits should be cut a lot or stopped for a carer on benefits who fails to attend an interview about finding work, 19 per cent of people on the left agree, 19 per cent of people in the centre agree and 21 per cent of people on the right agree. Far from being a source of political disagreement, it turns out that a similar (low) proportion of people across the political divide support sanctions in this case. These similarities, which are replicated for other groups of welfare recipients, might help to explain why there is currently a consensus between the main parties on welfare reform.[10]

WHEN PUSH COMES TO SHOVE

I want to pursue the question of how much people really care about personal responsibility. Some philosophers object to luck egalitarianism – the view that we should mitigate brute luck but hold people responsible for their voluntary choices – on the grounds that it is discontinuous with popular thinking. It is said that a blanket policy of refusing assistance to anyone who has made a bad choice or acted negligently would strike most people as harsh, unforgiving and unduly moralistic. Is this true? Not entirely. When asked about whether it is right to stop benefits for unemployed people, a whopping 78 per cent of respondents in Britain say that it would be right to limit a person's access if that they were not actively looking for work.[11] As I have already suggested, the British public are not particularly attracted to the idea of an unconditional right to unemployment benefits. These findings challenge the empirical basis for the objection that luck egalitarians are out of touch with popular thinking in Britain: for it appears that a very large majority of the British population do not suppose that withholding income payments to unemployed people is harsh, unforgiving or unduly moralistic. I dare say many people believe that far from it being harsh or cruel to withhold assistance it is cruel to maintain people on welfare benefits a day longer than is necessary, perhaps because the relationship demeans both the receiver and the giver.

This is not the end of the story, however. Although the British take a tough stance in relation to unemployed people, it remains the case that a majority of respondents, 55 per cent, say that benefits for lone parents should either be not affected or reduced a little if these people fail to attend interviews about finding work or training.[12] There may be a number of reasons for this attitude. One is that people don't want to appear heartless when interviewed by strangers. Another is that people don't want to see heavy sanctions against lone parents because of legitimate concerns for the children involved. Perhaps they see welfare benefits as being for the child rather than for the parent. Some people may take the view that although we should promote personal responsibility, stopping the benefits of lone parents is not a sensible way to achieve this end since it doesn't actually help these people to get out of the circumstances in which they find themselves. Still others may be convinced that it is usually better in terms of childhood development for the parent to stay at home. Some may be motivated by an overriding sense of compassion for parent and child or by a sense that making welfare benefits available to lone parents is a reasonable step given a lack of responsibility exercised by absent fathers.

So does this mean that fairness isn't people's number one priority after all? The short answer is that it's difficult to say. In his study bringing together evidence from a number of opinion studies, the British social scientist Peter Taylor-Gooby examines the level of public support for Miller's complex approach to social welfare provision. Miller's approach combines a social minimum ('All citizens must have access to resources that adequately meet their essential needs, and allow them to live a secure and dignified life in today's society') with fair distribution ('Resources that do not form part of equal citizenship or the social minimum may be distributed unequally, but the distribution must reflect relevant factors such as personal desert and personal choice').[13] Taylor-Gooby reports that although most people do care about the social minimum, they don't care about it a great deal, although they do care about it in the case of low income families and lone parents. Arguably in these cases there is a coming together of three things: support for a social minimum, a belief that these groups do make a fair contribution to society and concern about child poverty. There is, by contrast, much less support for a social minimum when it comes to people who are regarded as being lazy or as responsible for their own situations or as not giving anything back to society. This suggests that fairness, in the sense of holding adults responsible for the consequences of their actions, is important but not as important as alleviating child poverty.[14]

Turning to healthcare, this is one area of state spending where members of the public are much less willing to countenance the use of sanctions against irresponsible behaviour. One survey reveals that only 24 per cent of respondents say it would be right to limit a person's access to medical treatment under the NHS if their illness was due to a heavy smoking or drinking habit.[15] Why are people less likely to support sanctions in the case of medical treatment than in the case of access to health? One difference may be that people see healthcare as an issue of life and death and so they are more squeamish about denying treatment to people for irresponsible behaviour in this case. Then again, by this logic one might expect to see higher levels of public support for an unconditional basic income as a way of bringing people above the poverty line, given that severe poverty is often associated with inadequate nutrition, poor health and lower life expectancy.

Another difference may be that many people recognise they might fall into one of the categories of health irresponsibility during the course of their lives, whereas perhaps fewer people think they will ever need to claim unemployment benefits. (Of course, the latter number will increase during times of recession.) So an element of self-preservation might be lurking in these responses. If these conjectures are accurate, then in the case of healthcare we can say that concerns about fairness are superseded by a mixture of human compassion and self-preservation.

PERCEPTIONS AND REALITY

Understanding public attitudes is important, but it is equally important to identify possible gaps between public perceptions and the reality on the ground. If evidence from public opinion surveys is to play a role in testing normative theories of political arrangement, we must first get clear about how the relevant opinions are formed and the degree to which they are founded on truth or misconception. It should be no surprise to learn that there are mismatches between public perceptions about government spending and the true picture.

Consider once again the case of single parents. The 19th Report of the British Social Attitudes Survey (published in 2002) asked respondents to estimate the relative size of government social security spending on retirement pensions, children, benefits for disabled people, benefits for unemployed people and benefits for single parents. Interestingly, 35 per cent of the respondents assumed that spending on benefits for single parents was the largest or second largest amount of money spent on social security for these groups. However, the Report cites spending calculations from the Department for Work and Pensions showing that in reality benefits for single parents accounted for just 0.2 per cent of social security spending at that time. By far the largest proportion was the 67 per cent spent on retirement pensions. Perhaps if the public knew these facts, fewer people would be opposed to increased government spending on benefits for single parents.[16]

Another example of public confusion is the assumption that taxpayers have a right to social security benefits because there is a link between the benefits they receive and the contributions they make during the course of their working lives. Social security programmes in Britain indemnify people against disability, sickness and unemployment and, of course, provide retirement pensions. Since individuals pay towards these programmes through income tax and National Insurance contributions, many people feel that they have a strong entitlement to benefits. This is a matter of personal responsibility and fairness, as they see it, of making financial preparations for the future – albeit under the direction of the state – and of getting out what they have already paid in. So, for example, many people are strongly against means-testing of state pensions because they feel that a state pension is an inalienable right which they have bought through their contributions.[17]

This sort of attitude, however, is out of touch with the changing reality of social security in this country. John Hills, a Professor of Social Policy at the London School of Economics, maintains that although the principle of contribution has been a key part of the benefits system since the 1940s, there has been a decline in its impact. As he puts it: 'What we have is in fact a very weak contributory principle: benefits *mainly* depend on the fact of having made contributions, *but* people can receive "contributory benefits" without having made contributions, and can be ruled out of entitlement despite having made contributions.'[18] When access to benefits is severed from past contributions, responsibility inevitably slides away from the individual and falls into the lap of the rest of society. It is open to conjecture what people would say about social security programmes if they better understood that what individuals get out isn't necessarily what they put in.

Another interesting gap in public understanding comes to the fore when we ask the wealthiest people in our society about what it means to be poor. In 2008 Polly Toynbee and David Walker commissioned Ipsos MORI to interview a group of wealthy lawyers and bankers. Asked where the income poverty line currently falls in Britain they responded that it was at £22,000 per annum. In actuality, Toynbee and Walker calculate that the poverty line for a couple with children in Britain is £11,294. This suggests that wealthy people in Britain regard as poverty pay something that is in fact much closer to an average income.[19] Much less clear is whether this represents a kind of arrogant pity towards people living on £22,000 or genuine compassion for how hard it might be to live on that income. Asked about welfare claimants themselves, the views tended to be more regressive than progressive. One interviewee commented: 'Single people . . . get pregnant and get a flat and more money.'[20] Once again, however, the reality on the ground is rather different. The Welfare Act 2007 has made it a priority to increase the numbers of single mothers in employment, meaning that this group is now by and large expected to seek work along with the unemployed. As for the idea that single people can get pregnant and get a flat, the truth is that if a single mother needs a house in a hurry the chances are that she will receive low quality housing in an area with a history of anti-social problems. The higher the standard of housing a person wants, the longer he or she will have to wait for it.

There is also a perception in this country that the government spends a great deal of money on unemployment benefits. But all things are relative and Britain spends relatively little in comparison to other member countries of the Organisation for Economic Co-operation and Development (OECD). While Britain spent just 0.19 per cent of GDP on unemployment benefits in 2006, Germany spent a massive 2.04 per cent. The average across all member countries was 0.75 per cent of GDP.[21]

Social welfare is not the only arena of public policy where there is a gap between perception and reality. Take the widespread perception that smoking, alcoholism and obesity are public health issues in part because people with unhealthy lifestyles cost the country large sums of money in the extra burden they place on public health services. The reality is rather different, however. In fact economic studies show that the lifetime medical costs of looking after someone with a healthy lifestyle are in fact greater than those for people with obesity. Furthermore, the lifetime medical costs of looking after the obese are greater than the costs of looking after smokers. This is because people with healthy lifestyles on average live longer than obese people, who in turn live longer than smokers, and the longer people live the more expensive it becomes to treat them.[22] Of course, it is one thing to note the gap between perception and reality; it is quite another to say what would happen if the gap were closed. If the public understood the reality about the relative cost of smoking for public services, would they say that the government should break off efforts to encourage people to give up smoking? Perhaps not.

FURTHER INTERNATIONAL COMPARISONS

As one might expect, international social attitude surveys provide some interesting comparisons. The World Values Survey (1990–93) asked people from 71 countries whether they agree with the statement 'The government should take more responsibility to ensure that everyone is provided for' (1 meaning completely agree) versus the statement 'People should take more responsibility to provide for themselves' (10 meaning completely agree). Austria came out with the highest mean score of 7.5 and the US was ranked third. Here public attitudes clearly favour more personal responsibility. The Ukraine, by contrast, favoured much more government responsibility for social needs with a mean score of just over 3. Britain came in the middle with a mean of 5.5.[23]

Some of these results are easier to explain than others. It seems fairly obvious why people living in former Soviet states like the Ukraine would wish to see more government responsibility for social needs. Following the break-up of the Soviet Union in 1991 the Ukraine began the difficult transition from planned to free market economy. Since then the country has faced years of high unemployment and limited economic growth. Given these conditions no wonder the people of Ukraine want a safety-net. Conversely, there is a long tradition of antipathy towards 'large government' in the US which up until the current recession has seen decades of economic growth and relatively low levels of unemployment. Here the popular rhetoric is that individuals should receive a 'help up' rather than a 'hand out'. Some historians trace this ethos of personal responsibility and rugged individualism back to the pioneering spirit of the early American experience, where a culture of personal initiative and self-help was born out of geographical necessity and religious zeal.

The case of Sweden is more puzzling. Sweden comes out second in the order of ranking with very strong public support for more personal responsibility than it has now. This may seem surprising given the fact that the Social Democratic Party has dominated Swedish political life during most of twentieth century building a consensus across different sectors of society. In Sweden the welfare state is designed to integrate members of society and develop solidarity by providing a guaranteed minimum standard of living for all. So why is there now a popular desire to move towards greater personal responsibility? One answer has to do with rising levels of unemployment during the 1990s, which placed a strain on the permissive welfare system. Sweden spends a greater percentage of its national income on the welfare state than any other capitalist country. And it seems that Swedish taxpayers now feel as though they have paid enough.

As for the British, it would appear that they are more or less content with the current balance between government and personal responsibility. This is consistent with the earlier suggestion that most people support the present system of fair reciprocity in which the government has a responsibility to ensure that people have access to social assistance in times of hardship, but individuals also have a responsibility to seek work or training wherever possible. The upshot is that it would take a great deal of persuasion to get the British people to accept a drastic lurch towards either much higher levels of personal responsibility or much higher levels of government responsibility.

What about my claim that the British are much less in favour of penalising individuals for irresponsible behaviour in the area of health than in the area of social security? This also seems to be the case elsewhere in Europe. In 2005, for example, a group of social scientists conducted comparative research on attitudes towards personal responsibility in four European countries (France, Italy, Denmark and Sweden). A sample of 100 economics students in each country were asked whether it is fair for people's health premiums or contributions to be influenced by two main categories: circumstances (family medical background, for example) and personal choice (including diligence in taking medicine, eating or failing to eat a healthy diet, heavy smoking and participation in dangerous sporting activities). With respect to family medical background, 85 per cent of the respondents said that this factor should not increase people's premiums or contributions. In the case of unhealthy diet, 62 per cent said that this factor should not increase premiums or contributions, while 30 per cent favoured a 10 per cent increase. When it came to dangerous sports, 50 per cent said there should be no increase and 31 per cent preferred a 10 per cent increase. Only chain smokers were viewed more harshly, with 74 per cent recommending either a 10 or 30 per cent increase. According to the researchers, this evidence suggests that there is only weak public support in mainland Europe for the luck egalitarian principle that people's health premiums or contributions should not be sensitive to circumstances but should be sensitive to personal choices. Presumably if 100 per cent of people had said that family medical background should not increase health premiums or contributions and 100 per cent had said that poor nutrition, dangerous pastimes and chain smoking should increase health premiums or contributions, then the researchers would have presented this as evidence of strong support for the luck egalitarian principle.[24]

THE TROUBLE WITH OPINION SURVEYS

Having outlined some of the evidence from public opinions I now wish to offer a note of caution about this type of evidence. Opinion surveys provide a kind of raw data, but what the data tells us depends on who is asked, the way the questions are put and how researchers choose to interpret the answers. Take the study discussed in the previous paragraph. For one thing, it is uncertain how much can be read into the responses of economics students, since this is hardly a representative sample of the population as a whole. Furthermore, because the researchers started out with certain assumptions about which factors appropriately fall into the 'circumstances' and 'personal choice' categories respectively, the survey cannot be read as *revealing* how ordinary people make the cut between 'circumstances' and 'personal choice'. Some of the respondents might have queried the proposed chopping up if they had been given the opportunity to do so. So the results of the survey are ambiguous: either people are not especially sensitive to the circumstances/choice distinction or they are sensitive but they actually deem poor nutrition, risky pastimes and smoking habits to be matters of circumstances.

One solution to these problems lies in more qualitative and interactive examinations of what ordinary people think. This kind of research allows questioners to delve into the reasons why people have the attitudes they do. In other words, while opinion surveys are interesting up to a point, there is a need for greater interaction between the questioner and the respondent to ensure that they are interpreting each other correctly.

Some political philosophers have already set out along this path and the results are not entirely discouraging. In their 2007 book, *Disadvantage*, Jonathan Wolff and Avner de-Shalit conducted a series of one-to-one and group interviews of nearly 100 adults, including those who work with or who are themselves disadvantaged, in order to discover what it means to be disadvantaged, which disadvantages are most important and what should be done about them.[25] Interviewees were initially asked for their thoughts on what it means to be disadvantaged, but they were then given a showcard with a predetermined list of disadvantages written on it. At this point they were asked to pick out the three most important disadvantages and to say whether there was anything missing from the list. This list was drawn up by Wolff and de-Shalit based on a set of ten capabilities developed by another philosopher, Martha Nussbaum. According to the list, not being able to do or have the following things could amount to being disadvantaged: life, bodily health, bodily integrity, sense-imagination-thought, emotion, practical reason, affiliation, concern for other species, play and control over one's environment. To this Wolff and de-Shalit added: being able to do good for others, fidelity to the law, understanding the law and independence from others. Reflecting on the evidence, Wolff and de-Shalit concluded that life, bodily health, bodily integrity, affiliation, control over one's environment and sense-imagination-thought were deemed the most important by their interviewees.[26]

What was most interesting about their book, however, was its modification of Rawls' constructivist method of 'reflective equilibrium' – a method in which we test our pre-reflective beliefs about how a just society should be organised against our considered judgements about particular questions of justice. Reflection gives rise to a rough theory of justice and the reasoner goes back and forth adjusting both the initial beliefs and the considered judgements until there is a fit or equilibrium between them. To regard either as untouchable would be dogmatic.[27] But whereas Rawls conceived reflective equilibrium as more or less a private enterprise to be undertaken separately by himself and the readers of his books, Wolff and de-Shalit favour 'dynamic public reflective equilibrium'. The word 'dynamic' refers to the fact that they expect the list of disadvantages to change over time in response to what the interviewees say such that no result can be treated as more than provisional, while the word 'public' highlights the fact that philosophers are engaged in a process of reflection *with* the public.

Wolff and de-Shalit plan to commission more interviews in the future using a refined list of disadvantages. The new list will reflect the evidence collected to date – including the fact that many people from the original sample thought that being able to communicate in the dominant language of society was something missing from the list – and changes made in response to problems they foresee in applying/implementing the list in practice. Nevertheless, it remains the case that they began with a list of capabilities which *they* had selected. Of course, they had to start somewhere. It wouldn't have been feasible to discuss every possible type of disadvantage. But their selection comes at a price and that price is the right of the public to set the agenda in the first place. And this raises the following question: why not turn the tables? Rather than philosophers setting the agenda and interviewing members of the public, why not let members of the public set the agenda and do the interviewing?

In Chapter 8 I put the case for inviting members of the public to play a larger role in setting the agenda and participating in the deliberation as equals alongside philosophers, politicians and social policy experts and practitioners. I then develop a proposal for using citizens' juries as a way of turning the theory of democratic engagement into practice.

7   Four Contemporary Issues in Focus

The few observations I propose to make on questions of detail, are designed to illustrate the principles, rather than to follow them out to their consequences. I offer, not so much applications, as specimens of application.

John Stuart Mill

The central thrust of this book has been that personal responsibility matters, morally speaking, for a number of different reasons, but that the relative importance of these reasons is not well understood. As a result, the ideal of personal responsibility can be, and has been, used to justify a range of not necessarily consistent social policies. Before setting out the details of a procedure to arrive at determinate answers democratically, I want first to outline some pressing social issues and connected policy dilemmas which stand in need of some answers. I discuss these issues and dilemmas under four broad headings – unemployment, health, drug abuse and, finally, personal debt and financial rewards.

UNEMPLOYMENT

I need to make two things clear right away. The first is that unemployment is not the same as economic inactivity. The term 'unemployed' usually refers to people of working age who are without a job but available to start work, while 'economically inactive' signifies people who are not available to start work and are not actively seeking jobs, such as people with disabilities or who are retired or looking after children, spouses or elderly relatives. In the past public authorities in Britain tended to treat welfare claimants differently depending on whether they are unemployed or economically inactive, asking the former to seek work but allowing the latter to claim benefits without seeking work. As discussed in Chapter 5, however, the political wind has recently turned against some members of the latter group with increasing numbers of lone parents, for example, being switched from the category of economically inactive into the category of unemployed.

There is more than one possible justification for this. One has to do with fairness to taxpayers. It might be argued that in order to satisfy the demands of fair reciprocity lone parents should not merely bring up the next generation of workers but should also seek work and endeavour to get off welfare benefits at the earliest available opportunity. Another justification is that the label 'economically inactive' is not sensitive enough to capture the distinction between people who might want to work but feel trapped by their caring responsibilities and people who do not want to work or feel they can't work. Hence, regarding lone parents as ready and available for work may give expression to the concerns of those people who vehemently object to the way in which caring responsibilities tend to fall on women rather than men. Obviously it may not be possible to encourage and support every lone parent off benefits and into work, but that doesn't mean we shouldn't try.

This last observation brings me to my second clarification, which is that unemployment can be a structural problem. Marxists believe that unemployment is inevitable under the capitalist system because it always requires a reserve army of workers to help keep wages down. Whether or not this is strictly true, there is certainly a cyclical dimension to unemployment in most capitalist countries. Following the Wall Street crash of 1929 vast numbers of people didn't work because there simply weren't any jobs to be had. Such depressions are mercifully rare, but all economic downturns or recessions will have some impact on levels of unemployment and in ways that are beyond the control of ordinary individuals. Thus official unemployment figures in Britain and the US are currently the highest they have been since the recession of the early 1990s.[1] In times of economic gloom it becomes more difficult to blame individuals for their unemployment and policies designed to push people into work can seem cruel if there is less demand for labour and fewer jobs to be had. Nevertheless, I think that we must be careful to avoid the fallacy of explanatory structuralism: to falsely attribute all the causes of unemployment to the structure of the labour market thereby ignoring the role of personal responsibility. To be sure, structural unemployment can change people's behaviour and make them less inclined to seek work and more inclined to rely on benefits. But by the same token, people's behaviour can affect their chances of getting work in any economic circumstances.

If a government cannot cheerfully rely on people's innate sense of personal responsibility to find work whether in good or bad economic times, what else can and should it do? There are a range of financial sanctions available. One dates back to the Poor Laws. The principle of lesser eligibility says that the way to combat idleness and public dependency is to ensure that the standard of living of individuals who receive relief is never as good, or eligible, as the standard of living of individuals who support themselves through paid employment. The obvious drawback with this strategy, however, is that it will impoverish those who are not able to work just as much as those who can. Nor does it influence those who are perfectly willing to live a life of lesser eligibility.

A second strategy is to offer benefits only for a fixed period of time. This makes it clear from the start that assistance is only a temporary measure while people get themselves back on their feet after a change in circumstances such as redundancy. But this is another blunt instrument. If the automatic cut-off point is too long, it may offer some people an incentive to remain on the welfare rolls for longer than is strictly necessary. If it is too short, it will victimise individuals who are genuinely unable to find secure and lasting employment within the time limit. In fact, some welfare experts argue that cut-offs have a negligible impact on the work habits of the most recalcitrant. The American political scientist Lawrence M. Mead, for example, argues that the underlying problem of social dependency cannot be tackled with sanctions alone. 'Merely to deny aid does not tell people what they should be doing instead of being dependent. It is not prescriptive enough.'[2] According to Mead, the answer to the problem is to make access to benefits conditional on job-search behaviour. His main justification for workfare is not an argument of fairness, however, but a paternalistic argument about the beneficial results it has for the material and psychological well-being of the poor.[3]

Half a century after the 1942 Beveridge Report, the late John Smith MP, Tony Blair's predecessor as leader of the Labour Party, established a Commission to look at issues of social justice in Britain. The Commission also proposed workfare as a new core strategy for dealing with unemployed people. The proposal was that 'someone who unreasonably turns down a job or a training offer cannot expect to continue claiming full benefits'.[4]

Influenced inter alia by the Commission on Social Justice the Labour government rolled out the New Deal in 1998. The New Deal is a programme in which claimants sign a contract agreeing to take up suitable employment or training as a condition of receiving Jobseeker's Allowance. In the case of the New Deal for Young People, which has received the lion's share of funding to date, there is an initial 'gateway' session organised by the Jobcentre Plus office designed to improve the claimant's job-searching and interview skills. If the search for employment remains unsuccessful, the claimant will be offered one or more of the following choices: a job placement, full-time education or training, work in the voluntary sector or with the Environmental

Task Force. If a claimant refuses all 'reasonable' offers of work or training, he or she will be sanctioned by having benefits stopped for 1, 2, 4 or 26 weeks. If someone's Jobseeker's Allowance stops, then his or her Housing Benefit and Council Tax Benefit also stops.[5]

Defenders of the New Deal from within the Labour Party claim that it provides opportunity but also encourages personal responsibility: not only does it force people to be more proactive in looking for work or improving their own skills but it also holds persons responsible for their actions if they refuse to abide by the rules. This to some extent mirrors justifications for workfare found in the liberal egalitarian literature. One such argument claims that withholding benefits from those who elect not to seek employment is one way of holding them personally responsible for their voluntary choices. A second argument appeals to fairness as reciprocity. It says that people who wish to enjoy the benefits of social cooperation must do something in return and this means at the very least searching for work. A third argument draws on the contractualist tradition in political philosophy that the principle of workfare would be a feature of the social welfare regime that individuals would agree to under idealised conditions of freedom and equality. According to Dworkin's version of this argument, we should imagine that we all have the same antecedent chance of being made redundant and the same opportunity to purchase insurance policies against that risk. He argues that the most popular insurance policies would be those according to which policyholders are required to pursue job training as a condition of receiving any payouts. People would prefer these policies because the premiums would be cheaper.[6]

These arguments provide a good starting point but they are very far from complete. What, more exactly, constitutes a reasonable level of job-searching behaviour? Does a redundant computer programmer act unreasonably by declining work as an office cleaner? Is it really the case that placed under imaginary conditions of equality we would want to purchase such insurance policies? Wouldn't many of us choose something that offers more flexibility? Furthermore, just how suitable is workfare in straightened economic circumstances? When US President Franklin D. Roosevelt championed the New Deal for the American people during the 1930s he included emergency relief programmes designed to help poor unemployed people survive the Great Depression. The Labour government's New Deal, by contrast, included welfare reforms to push welfare claimants back into work in times of relative prosperity. But now we find ourselves in difficult economic circumstances again with rising unemployment and fewer jobs. So is workfare still the right policy?

Even if answers to these questions could be found, however, stacked up against the arguments in favour of workfare are a range of ethical considerations which point in a very different direction. One is that work requirements place all of the bargaining power in the hands of officials and those companies offering the training programmes and the jobs. So unless the government is prepared to regulate these programmes quite heavily, participants may end up feeling as though they are being exploited. Indeed, the New Deal has been criticised in some quarters for the low pay and poor quality of its mandatory jobs and training schemes and for the limited success people have had in securing permanent employment.[7] A related concern is that participants in New Deal programmes have been given a bad name before they even show up for work. The Commission on Social Justice, for example, found some evidence to suggest that employers were reluctant to employ individuals whom they perceived to be unwilling conscripts.[8]

. A further potential problem is the adverse impact that taking lone parents out of the category of economically inactive and into the category of unemployed jobseekers might have on their dependants. Here the debate about personal responsibility must be situated in the context of a larger debate about parental responsibility. Anyone who favours rules or policies that have the aim of getting more lone parents back into work must answer the following questions. Is it better or worse for the child not to have a parent at home looking after him or her? What happens if some parents refuse to play ball and lose their benefits? In the words of George Will, 'No child is going to be spiritually improved by being collateral damage in a bombardment of severities targeted at adults who may or may not deserve more severe treatment from the welfare system.'[9]

The threat to childhood development is not the only potential side-effect of workfare policies. The state must also recognise the issues of invasion of privacy and shameful revelation discussed in previous chapters. One response to these alleged weaknesses might be to challenge the empirical foundations on which they are built. Couldn't the state make better use of information that is either already in the public domain or that is easily obtainable without intrusion or shameful revelation? Census data, electoral registers, identity cards, national insurance, medical records – perhaps these are information streams that could be harnessed to assess some claims without the need to interview people face to face. Then again, it is hard to know how this would actually work in practice. The state would still need to gather the relevant information at some point during the course of a person's life. Even if some individuals are willing to volunteer this information and give permission for that information to be shared across government departments, other individuals will strongly object. Moreover, in some cases the information may pertain to children and it may be just as shameful for parents to publicly declare certain facts about their children as it is for adults to publicly declare certain facts about themselves.

A more salutary point is that individuals may be more willing to volunteer information under a regime in which they can present not just facts about their capacity to work but also evidence about why they live as they do, their reciprocal contributions to society, their deservingness, and so on. Rather than seeing the exploration of this larger ethical story as intrusive or shameful, people might come to see it as a way for the state to show respect for who they really are. For example, someone might be happy to explain that she is unemployed because she cares for an elderly parent to whom she is deeply devoted or that she is a stay at home mother because she passionately believes this is the right thing to do or that she wouldn't trust the childminders in her area with her dog let alone her child. This underlines once again, I think, the need for greater public engagement in social policy decision-making so that authorities understand the sorts of information people are comfortable offering.

Issues of equality and diversity raise further complications. Researchers are increasingly interested in the values that stand behind social policies and whether or not they reflect society as a whole or merely the dominant group or culture. They have become very adept at pointing out ways in which current policies fail to respect cultural diversity. Bandana Ahmad, for example, highlights the case of a girl in Britain who was compelled by her respite carers to wear her nightdress during the day because they didn't know how to dress her in her 'ethnic clothing'. Similarly, in her 1988 book, *Social Policy: A Critical Introduction*, Fiona Williams argues that historically social policy has been dominated by a certain model of the 'normal' citizen. The upshot is that social services have favoured a certain type of family structure, the welfare state has been geared up to assisting those with a stable work record, and public provision of social housing and primary healthcare has discriminated against non-citizens.[10]

The basic message coming out of this work is that social policies must respect the fact of equality and diversity. This is by no means a bad line of thought, but it is one that raises as many questions as it answers. Consider once again the New Deal programme. In ordinary circumstances if a claimant refuses to take up suitable employment or training he or she will be sanctioned by having his or her Jobseeker's Allowance stopped. However, under regulation 73 of the Jobseeker's Allowance Regulations 1996 sanctions cannot be imposed if someone has 'good cause' for refusal. The regulations set out a number of exemptions including that 'the claimant's failure to participate in the training scheme or employment programme resulted from a religious or conscientious objection sincerely held.'[11] Commissioners working in this area are charged with the task of applying the regulations. They have accepted that a Christian who refused to work on Sundays had good cause for voluntarily leaving his employment as did a Jewish claimant who refused to work on Saturdays. Some secular objections have also been accommodated, such as a vegetarian who refused work as a secretary for a company which manufactured sausages and meat pies. But in another important test case a different sort of objection was not accepted and this is what I want to explore now.

In 1998 a welfare claimant (call him Mr X) who had been in receipt of Jobseeker's Allowance since 1997 was informed that he was to be enrolled on a 'Jobplan workshop' run by a commercial agency which was the only provider of such programmes in his area. The claimant refused on principled grounds. He wrote to the manager of his Jobcentre stating, 'I decline to countenance a scheme organised by a private, profit driven, company which clearly involves exposure of my personal details to a limited company.' A two week disqualification from Jobseeker's Allowance was imposed by an adjudicating official. Mr X appealed against that decision, but a tribunal dismissed his appeal. However, its chairman observed that the meaning of 'conscientious objection' was a matter of surmise and indicated that leave to appeal would be granted if sought. Mr X duly appealed and at the re-hearing in November 2000 a new tribunal (consisting of one district chairman) dismissed his appeal. A second leave to appeal was refused in May 2001. Then in October 2001 Commissioner E. A. L. Bano granted leave to appeal once again, and he was tasked by the Secretary of State to make a decision on that appeal. Finally, in September 2002 Commissioner Bano ruled that Mr X's objection did not fall into the category of a religious or conscientious objection. His main justification was this:

A principled objection is not the same as a conscientious objection, and although the claimant objects to the provision of employment programmes by private organisations and to the disclosure of his personal details to a private company, he has not stated that his attendance at the training course would have required him personally to act in a way which was contrary to his ethical or moral principles. I therefore do not consider that the claimant's reasons for not attending the training programme amounted to a conscientious objection.[12]

What I find most troubling about this ruling – other than the astonishing length of time devoted to appeals and the obvious cost implications for taxpayers – is the way in which a 'principled objection' is summarily regarded as inferior to a religious or conscientious objection. Assuming that principled objections can be just as sincerely held as religious or conscientious objections, what is the argument for such a differentiation? Besides, what exactly is a principled objection? It may well be that Commissioner Bano decided the case correctly in accordance with existing regulations. But the deeper issue is whether or not the underlying regulation is correct. Why should the class of exemptions be limited to religious or conscientious objections? Doesn't this discriminate against people whose sincerely held principles do not fall neatly into these categories? In a society of equality and diversity, why should we favour conscience over principle?

No doubt some people will deem that Mr X had a weak argument in the first place. Even if they concede his sincerity, they will insist that it does not constitute a genuine cost in liberty to have one's information passed on to a private employment agency. It might even be pointed out that Mr X's objection to the private agency was undermined by the fact that he was claiming unemployment benefits funded through general taxation – taxation which relies on the existence of a profit-driven economy. They will say that if such objections were permitted, this would make a mockery of the New Deal. But other reasonable people may take a different view. They might think that even welfare claimants have a right to privacy. They may recognise Mr X's principled view that social welfare programmes ought to be handled within the public as opposed to private sector irrespective of where the money comes from. Indeed, they might share Mr X's belief that all forms of profiteering are morally wrong and taxes should not be collected on the back of such a system. Or they might simply take the view that society should try to be neutral with regard to different kinds of objections; provided, of course, these are reasonable objections. As with most questions of social policy, there needs to be a line drawn somewhere between what is reasonable and what is not. So the question is: who should be responsible for drawing up the list of approved objections?

HEALTH

Health raises its own questions of personal responsibility. It is impossible to meet every medical need, to the fullest degree, at any given moment. Doing so would cost too much money and even if we had the money, we might prefer to spend it on other things. Consequently, Britain has seen the withdrawal of certain kinds of treatments – cosmetic surgery and some fertility treatment, for example – as free services under the NHS. These services are, in effect, regarded as matters of personal choice rather than strict medical need. But who is to decide what constitutes a matter of personal choice? And what role, if any, should there be for public consultation in these decisions?

Questions of personal responsibility also emerge in relation to the allocation of such things as organ transplants and joint operations. Philosophers are fond of examples that test our intuitions about personal responsibility. Take the imaginary case of a doctor who must decide between giving the only available hospital bed to a drunk driver or to the innocent pedestrian he knocked down.[13] The General Medical Council, however, who are in charge of setting the professional standards by which the medical profession must operate in Britain, explicitly state in their guidance to doctors that personal responsibility is *not* a suitable basis for making resource allocation decisions:

> The investigations or treatment you provide or arrange must be based on the assessment you and the patient make of their needs and priorities, and on your clinical judgement about the likely effectiveness of the treatment options. You must not refuse or delay treatment because you believe that a patient's actions have contributed to their condition. You must treat your patients with respect whatever their life choices and beliefs.[14]

The reality on the ground can be somewhat different, however. To take just one example, in 2005 various NHS trusts in Suffolk decided not to perform knee surgery on people with a Body Mass Index of over 30. They claimed that the decision was based on the person being unlikely to benefit from the procedure in question. Yet subsequent studies have shown that having a BMI of over 30 does not actually limit the benefits of knee replacement.[15] This raises suspicion about the real criteria standing behind these sorts of policies and practices. Doctors and healthcare trusts may claim until they are blue in the face that they do not allocate on the basis of personal responsibility, but if recovering alcoholics are consistently passed over for liver transplants and obese people are denied knee surgery, it is hard to avoid drawing the conclusion that covert responsibility judgements are in play, whether that is a judgement about the sort of behaviour which may have contributed to someone's condition or a judgement about whether or not the patient can be trusted to act responsibly in following doctor's orders after treatment.[16]

At this stage, however, some readers might be thinking that there is an obvious solution to these issues. The government could simply make it a legal requirement that people who run certain types of risk either make additional contributions to the government insurance scheme or purchase a minimum amount of insurance from approved commercial companies. Governments could even increase taxes on cigarettes, alcohol and fast foods and use that revenue to fund the relevant medical treatments. These policies deserve consideration, but they also throw up additional ethical questions. One has to do with a cost in autonomy. Even if compulsory insurance programmes and ring-fenced taxes help to ensure that people have access to the healthcare they will probably need in the future, which in turn protects their long-term autonomy, this does limit autonomy in the short term, since it denies people's freedom of choice to take an uninsured risk.

On the other hand, governments often impose rules which require individuals to minimise the risk of serious injury or death and by and large the population are willing to accept these rules because they recognise, perhaps in their more reflective moments, their own carelessness or weakness of will. Consider rules which forbid people from swimming in public pools or at public beaches when lifeguards are not present. There is nothing disrespectful about this paternalism (so the argument goes) because it appeals to people's self-awareness of what is in their own best interests. So from the mere fact that something is paternalistic it doesn't follow that it is unjustified. The question is whether any given piece of paternalism amounts to a reasonable trade-off between present and future autonomy. Perhaps asking smokers to contribute to an insurance scheme for smoking-related diseases is no worse than asking people to contribute to a pension scheme for retirement. It is certainly less paternalistic than banning smoking outright. But once again this is a matter about which reasonable people can disagree. That such policies involve an autonomy trade-off is hard to deny. The difficult question is what kind of trade-off is the most reasonable one to make.

In Chapter 6 I pointed to evidence suggesting that people with unhealthy lifestyles in fact place a lesser cost on public health services than people with healthy lifestyles because of their lower relative life expectancy. Putting the problem this way forces us to consider why we really care about personal responsibility in relation to health. If the only reason why we care about healthy lifestyles is to reduce the tax burden on others, then arguably the government should *stop* encouraging people to eat more healthily, take regular exercise, stop smoking, and so on. But few people seriously think that this is the right thing to do, and this may be because we care about healthy lifestyles for reasons other than fairness.

At any rate, much thinking needs to be done about the best allocation of preventive responsibilities. What rights do patients have to screening programmes and public health campaigns funded by the government? Conversely, what preventive responsibilities should fall on patients themselves? Standing behind the new NHS constitution is the assumption that since no affordable health scheme can cover every treatment for every possible sickness, prevention must be the best policy. In this way the question of prevention is recast as a question of reciprocity: while individuals have a right to public provision of preventive health programmes, the state has a right to demand healthy living from individuals. But does the new constitution achieve a fair balance of rights and responsibilities? Does having a catalogue of patients' responsibilities leave enough space for people to exercise their own judgement about how to live well?

Once a government has decided to emphasise preventive responsibility, it also faces the question of how to promote this end. What is best – the carrot or the stick? The stick involves issuing a command and backing it up with sanctions, which typically leaves individuals with little room for manoeuvre. In the case of healthcare, the ultimate sanction is the denial of treatment. The carrot, by contrast, works by offering people positive incentives. Few countries have done more to incentivise healthy living than Germany. Its Social Security Code (SGB) sets out both the responsibilities and incentives of the statutory health insurance scheme. Among other things, it specifies that medical services must be called upon by patients only when necessary and that patients must make additional contributions for medical treatment resulting from criminal activity, self-harm, cosmetic surgery, tattoos and body piercing. But it also states that financial incentives can be paid to those people who agree to take part in screening, check-up and managed care programmes, or who do not use general practitioners or hospital services for a given period of time.[17]

The German model raises a number of interesting moral questions. For example, if financial incentives were instituted in Britain, might they actually have the perverse effect of making some people less healthy because they prefer to receive the cash bonus than see a doctor? If poorer patients are more likely to avoid seeing the doctor so that they can get the cash bonus than wealthier patients, won't the policy make the problem of health inequality worse in this country? How can this be fair? Besides, what about people who are genetically predisposed to various illnesses and cannot avoid seeing doctors on a regular basis? In effect, they will be penalised for being unhealthy. The policy seems to assume conditions of background equality of opportunity for health that don't actually exist. Moreover, what do the financial incentives say about the state's view of its own citizens? Are they symbolic of the fact that the state does not consider us to be capable of judging for ourselves what kind of life we would like to live, what screening and medical services we think are worthwhile and at what risk to our own life expectancy?

DRUG ABUSE

Another set of dilemmas emerge in respect of drug policy. No debate about the problem of drug abuse can take place without first acknowledging the economic and social costs of addiction. To explore these costs is not to condone drug use but to see the world as it actually is. According to a Home Office Research Study for the year 2000, the total economic cost of Class A drug use for that year, including emergency health services, spending on drug treatment programmes, criminal justice and social welfare costs, was estimated as £3.5 billion. Adding victims' costs and the loss of economic productivity caused by individual impairment or premature death, the total estimated economic and social costs were £12 billion. This equates to £6,564 for each Class A user, and £35,456 for problem users, responsible for the majority of costs. (The latter group includes people who inject heroin and regular long-term users of cocaine, crack and amphetamines.) According to an estimate from 2004–05, there are 327,000 problem drug users in England alone. Other studies estimate that a third of problem users are in treatment, a third have previously been in treatment and a third have never been in treatment.[18]

The Labour government's drugs strategy has been to try to increase the numbers of problem drug users in treatment, with increased referrals through the criminal justice system where appropriate, and to significantly increase year on year the proportion of users successfully completing treatment programmes. The 2004 Public Service Agreement (PSA) on illegal drugs set the target of a 100 per cent increase in the number of problem drug users in treatment by 2008. Having made headway in achieving this target, the new ten-year drug strategy rolled out in March 2008 commits the government to further increases. Other plans include more neighbourhood policing, targeting problem drug users who cause the highest level of crime, improving prison treatment programmes, increasing the use of community sentences with a drug rehabilitation requirement, strengthening and extending international agreements to intercept drugs being trafficked into Britain, extending powers to seize the cash and assets of drug dealers, intervening early in families with parents who use drugs in order to prevent harm to children and using the benefits system to compel people to enter into drug treatment programmes.[19]

The last measure is particularly interesting. The proposal is to empower Jobcentre Plus officers to refer drug users to specialist treatment providers as a condition of receiving benefits. According to some estimates, around 50,000 people who are claiming Incapacity Benefit are problem drug users, and while there are no plans to apply the proposals retrospectively, the new proposals may affect 4,000 new claimants a year. Under the new policy: 'In return for benefit payments, claimants will have a responsibility to move successfully through treatment and into employment.'[20]

What should we make of this policy? One immediate thought is that it is a bit like the old Christian test for identifying witches. A person is asked to 'move successfully through treatment and into employment'. If worthy, the person will get off drugs and into work. If not worthy, the treatment programme won't work for him. So if he succeeds in the programme, he is no longer entitled to benefits. And if he fails in the programme, he is no longer enti- tled to benefits. Either way, the person ends up without benefits.

No doubt some people will say that any proposal to get more people enrolled on drug treatment programmes must be a good thing; provided, that is, it works and offers good value for money. Looking at the figures, however, doesn't make for encouraging reading on either score. Despite a £131 million boost in funding for the National Treatment Agency and an estimated 195,000 people in drug treatment in 2007, the numbers of people who emerge from treatment drug-free only increased from 5,759 in 2004 to 5,829 in 2007. This means that the proportion of users emerging drug-free is still only 3 per cent. As one commentator puts it, 'This amounts to an increase of only 70 more people, a hefty price tag of £1.85m for each addict to get clean.'[21]

Of course, the government will argue that one cannot expect immediate results from the additional spending and that a 130 per cent increase of people in drug treatment programmes between 1998 and 2007 is an important step in the right direc- tion. Be that as it may, the reason for the increase in spending on drug treatment programmes cannot be measured purely in financial terms. Indeed, if the *only* rationale were to reduce economic and social costs, then one radical strategy would be to simply redirect all of the money that the government currently spends on treatment programmes and use it to increase drug seizures and prosecutions against middle-market drug dealers, and to curb heroin production in Afghanistan and imported drugs from around the world. Since the largest proportion of government spending on the drug problem is devoted to criminal justice costs and drug enforcement, an even more radical strategy would be to simply legalise Class A drugs. Although medical costs of treating problem drug users and social costs associated with drug-related crimes and loss of productivity would stay the same or increase, the Chancellor of the Exchequer could introduce a new tax regime in order to pay for this reactive expenditure. In the current political climate, however, it is unlikely that any of the major political parties could hope to win an election while promising to legalise Class A drugs. For example, a survey of British social attitudes to drugs in 2002 found that only 6 per cent of respondents believed that cannabis should be legalised and just 1 per cent thought that ecstasy and heroin should be legalised.[22]

In fact, the government has offered four main justifications for increasing spending on drug treatment programmes. First, the government declares that it wants to be fair to taxpayers. Second, it wants to protect children whose parents are problem drug users. Third, it wants to clean up neighbourhoods. Fourth, it wants people to flourish as human beings. It is possible to interpret each of these reasons as reasons of personal responsibility (both reflexive and non-reflexive). First, it is not fair to force taxpayers simply to support problem drug users when they could be getting treatment to overcome their addictions. Second, in an ideal world all children would have access to good parenting, meaning that all parents would be able to assume responsibility for the welfare of their own children. Third, individuals should not be permitted to make the lives of other people within a community uncomfortable or dangerous. Fourth, a flourishing life is one in which people are able to take control of their own lives and look after themselves through work. Alongside lack of education, mental health problems and disability, drug or alcohol dependency is another major barrier to work.

However, these reasons may not be as consistent as they first appear. Suppose someone has become a heroin addict and cannot blame anyone else for his situation since he voluntarily chose to start injecting. According to one interpretation of fairness, because he is responsible for the mess in which he finds himself, it would be wrong to force taxpayers to pay for his mistakes by funding drug treatment. Yet if we believe that being able to take control of one's personal ends is an essential part of what it means to lead a good life, we may not wish to abandon the addict to his stupor. If we wish to see him recover his capacity for responsible agency, in other words, we may believe that taxpayers' money should be spent on the specialist treatment he needs. So it looks as though we have an unavoidable conflict of values. On the one hand, we want addicts to recover their capacity for personal responsibility. But on the other hand, we want to be fair to taxpayers. So what should we do?

Perhaps it might be possible to partially avoid this conflict by concentrating on a different conception of fairness. Fairness can be construed as a matter of appropriately holding persons responsible for the consequences of their actions. Thus if a person is causally responsible for becoming an addict, then he cannot fairly expect our assistance in getting off drugs. But suppose instead we view fairness as a matter of what drug addicts can do in return for assistance now and in the future. This is fairness as reciprocity. We might introduce an element of community service into drug treatment programmes such that as part of the treatment persons are required to engage in projects that 'give something back to their society'. Consider a drug treatment centre located in a local farm which produces food for the local community and provides days out for young people to see the farm and meet former addicts. Obviously this still leaves the thorny question of how governments decide what kinds of reciprocal contributions are appropriate and how much taxpayers' money to spend on these sorts of schemes. But at the very least this seems to be a way of combining fairness with other values. I call this a 'partial' solution to the conflict of values, however, because there are bound to be individuals who continuously break the rules of such programmes and there may come a point at which withdrawing access to expensive treatment becomes the fairest thing to do as far as the taxpayer is concerned.

There is a further dimension to this issue not yet considered. Given the immense difficulty and cost of getting people off drugs once they are already hooked on them, common sense would seem to dictate that what is needed here is a more preventive approach. Rather than devoting all the available resources to drug treatment, more money should be spent on information campaigns and education programmes in schools to prevent people becoming addicts in the first place, and on providing people with meaningful alternatives to a life of drug abuse. If we value personal responsibility as a way of life, let us put the investment into making young people understand the threat that drugs pose to that way of life. Once again, however, we need some reliable way of knowing how much of its resources the government should devote to preventive policies. If the government devotes too much to prevention, it risks abandoning existing addicts. Not enough and it will be left with the problem of drug abuse for generations to come.

PERSONAL DEBT AND FINANCIAL REWARDS

One of the most conspicuous ways in which people nowadays fail to take personal responsibility for their own lives is by racking up large personal debts which they are unable to repay. According to Credit Action, a UK-based charity which offers free debt counselling advice, the average debt in the UK for households with some form of unsecured loan (excluding mortgages) is £21,875. This figure increases to £59,670 if mortgages are included. The interest alone paid on average by each household in respect of their total debt is estimated at £3,774 each year.[23]

Of course, many people will find themselves with unmanageable debts because they are living below the poverty line and cannot make ends meet or because of an unforeseen change of personal circumstances such as the break-up of a marriage, illness or redundancy. But some people are in this predicament because of high consumption, gratuitous spending and the failure to delay gratification.

What is to be done about this sort of irresponsibility? Few people nowadays would endorse the code of law created by Genghis Khan to deal with debtors, according to which the death penalty was mandated for anyone who became bankrupt three times. In direct contrast to this, the Christian perspective on debt emphasises both personal responsibility and forgiveness. The message to the debtor is that it is a sin to borrow money and never repay it (Psalm 37: 21). As for the creditor, the message is one of gracious forbearance. Hence, the Old Testament prescribes that one 'Holy Year' or 'Jubilee Year' should take place every half century when there is a remission of debts and debt-slaves are freed by heavenly command (Leviticus 25: 8–54). The book of Moses also contains plenty of examples of the cancellation of debt by creditors as an instance of compassionate treatment of the poor (Deuteronomy 15: 1–2).

Even if forgiveness and compassion are suitable for some people's personal lives, however, the question is whether or not political authorities have a moral right to be so forgiving. The point is that in today's largely secular society only a minority of people actively hold to Christian views on jubilee remission, so it is far from obvious that the government would act legitimately if it unilaterally decided to force banks to cancel debts. Libertarians, for example, will urge that helping debtors is rightly a matter for private individuals, charities and commercial companies to pursue as their consciences dictate, but it is not something the state should foist upon taxpayers without their consent.

British citizens who find themselves with unmanageable debt can file for 'voluntary bankruptcy' which enables them to walk away from most of their debt and repay creditors in an orderly manner. In addition to this, the Insolvency Act 1986 makes provision for individuals with debt problems to enter into Individual Voluntary Arrangements (IVAs) with their creditors. IVAs typically run for five years after which time any outstanding balances are written off and the debtor is free to make a fresh start. According to some estimates, the average IVA debtor owes £52,000 but is seeking to repay only around 40 per cent of this sum. While IVAs may yield significantly less than the original debt, they can be an attractive alternative to bankruptcy in the eyes of creditors, since the fees associated with bankruptcy are high and there can be little or no assets to be sought. It is estimated that one person in the UK becomes bankrupt or enters into an IVA every three and a half minutes.[24]

Although the voluntary aspect of the IVA expresses a kind of personal responsibility, in the sense of owning up to one's own mistakes, someone who enters into an IVA nevertheless evades the full consequences of the life he or she has lived. Taking this step is a way of mitigating some of the costs, but the majority of the costs still fall on the lending institutions and that institution will either pass these costs on to their customers or reduce payouts to shareholders. In so far as the costs are ultimately borne by other people either in the form of higher bank charges or lower dividends, it may seem unfair that debtors can get into financial difficulty through the most irresponsible behaviour and then make a fresh start after just five years. Indeed, it might be argued that IVAs almost encourage irresponsible behaviour.

So how can we make the system fairer? One possibility is more state regulation of lenders, borrowers and the IVA industry. One strategy is for the government to force banks and building societies to restrict the amount of money they lend to individuals and under what terms and conditions. Another is tighter restrictions on the licensed Insolvency Practitioners (IPs) who prepare the

IVAs. One strategy has been to ban IPs from using daytime TV and internet advertising to drum up business. It may also be appropriate to mandate longer repayment periods, so that people cannot so easily evade their debt. A deeper issue here is whether or not commercial companies should be allowed to profit from bad debt in this way. If profiteering runs contrary to principles of fairness or to the public interest, there may be a case for nationalising the IVA industry. Nevertheless, one thing all of these instruments have in common is that they limit people's freedom to act in ways that impose unfair burdens on others.

Another possibility is to leave the legislation more or less as it stands and let the market find its own equilibrium. The number of IVAs in Britain increased sharply from fewer than 5,000 in 1998 to an estimated 45,000 in 2006. This is in addition to the 65,000 people who were declared bankrupt in 2006. Given the underlying problem of irresponsible debt, it seems likely that the numbers of people seeking IVAs will continue to increase over the coming years. However, in 2007 major lenders such as HSBC started to resist some of the more generous remissions requested by IPs. This new tougher stance along with increasing competition within the IVA industry and intervention by the government against aggressive advertising campaigns caused a profit warning and slump in share prices of Debt Free Direct and other leading providers of IVAs.[25] So there are signs that the pendulum is beginning to swing back in the direction of more modest IVA settlements and this may be a fairer outcome. The only problem here is if the pendulum swings too far in the other direction and people are unable to make reasonable IVA arrangements with banks. This may encourage people to abrogate even more personal responsibility by filing for bankruptcy.

For all of these reasons I think that it is appropriate for the government to check and double-check that its policies in this area include the perspectives of ordinary people. What are the right priorities when it comes to personal debt? Drawing on the moral values discussed throughout this book, we can ask the following question: what is the relative importance of preventing individuals from unfairly imposing burdens on other people and respecting people's autonomy to make their own financial mistakes?

Thus far I have concentrated on the personal responsibility of low income earners and borrowers. It is now time to focus on high income earners and lenders. After all, one of the central architects of the Third Way, Anthony Giddens, argued that the principle of rights and responsibilities should apply not merely to welfare recipients but also to rich taxpayers, to corporations and to politicians themselves. Everyone who benefits from social cooperation must give back to the community.[26]

Arguably many of the problems we are now facing in the economy stem from the fact that this isn't what happened in practice. Some companies and super-rich individuals have paid proportionately low tax, sometimes because of illegal activity (tax evasion) and sometimes because of a low tax burden imposed by the government (tax avoidance). More generally, high-flyers in the banking sector have engaged in all manner of gratuitous risk-taking, over-pricing and financial flimflammery – none of which can be tolerably described as responsible in a larger ethical sense. The lack of regulation of the financial sector has left many people to reflect on the bitter irony of the avowedly 'prudent' Gordon Brown who recently proclaimed with reference to the banking crisis the end of 'the age of irresponsibility'. Wasn't it Brown himself who oversaw and implicitly endorsed this irresponsibility as Chancellor?[27]

Given the wealth accumulated by an elite band of super-rich tax evaders, private-equity capitalists, unscrupulous lenders, white collar fraudsters and city fat cats who command massive bonuses, the question we should perhaps be asking ourselves is why as a society we have become so fixated on the responsibilities of the poor and have lost sight of the responsibilities of the rich. Perhaps the answer lies in the fact that as a society we were led to believe three propositions about the economy, each of which now seems untrue.

The first proposition was that because talented high-flyers are personally responsible for generating wealth, they are entitled to reap their rewards no matter how large the rewards become. Philosophically, this proposition was severely weakened by Rawls when, in *A Theory of Justice*, he described the distribution of talents as 'arbitrary from a moral perspective'. He pointed out that 'Even the willingness to make an effort, to try, and so to be deserving in an ordinary sense is itself dependent upon happy family and social circumstances.'[28] Obviously it is one thing to say that this proposition has been discredited from a philosophical point of view; it is quite another to say that it lacks popular support. Ideas about just deserts still dominate public opinion when it comes to earnings. In his book, *Principles of Social Justice*, Miller cites one survey of British social attitudes where 95 per cent of respondents agreed with the statement 'People who work hard deserve to earn more than those who do not'. What is much less clear, however, is why people are willing to agree to these sorts of statements. Miller conjectures that this may have more to do with people's realisation that the economic system depends on the payment of incentives to the talented than with a commitment to just deserts as a key principle of economic morality.[29] But then this raises another ethical question. Why should talented people demand extremely high salaries before they will contribute to society? Wouldn't it be fairer to the rest of society if they had a more egalitarian ethos?[30]

The second thing we were led to believe was that by leaving people in the financial sector to their own devices economic growth could go on for ever. This claim has crumbled under the weight of the recession. Few people now seriously think that the best way to ensure year on year growth is to turn a blind eye to what happens in the city. It is widely believed that it was irresponsible behaviour in the financial sector, including irresponsible lending on mortgages and unsecured personal loans and credit cards, that caused the current economic bust and every day more and more governments around the world are drawing up plans to regulate and oversee that sector more closely.

The third proposition was that super-rich tax evaders and white collar fraudsters don't really cost us anything. This has also been shown to be a myth, since selfish behaviour by these people means that ordinary citizens wind up losing their savings or paying higher taxes. There are some famous examples. Take the rogue traders Nick Leeson and Jerome Kerviel who lost their banks an estimated $1.3bn and $7.1bn respectively. Or else consider the American hedge fund manager Bernard Madoff who is alleged to have lost $50bn of his customers' money, including major banks and local authorities. The US Federal Government also recently indicted Joe Francis, the porn magnate, on two counts of tax evasion relating to $20m concealed in offshore accounts. Of course, there are hundreds of less well-known examples of individuals taking reckless gambles with pension funds or evading taxes with offshore accounts which together add up to vast sums of money, all of which imposes economic burdens on ordinary people.[31]

Assuming the above picture is accurate, what should governments do about these problems? First, many people are calling on the government either to force banks to self-regulate their bonus schemes or to regulate bonuses directly. But what could justify this step from a moral point of view and what constitutes an excessive or unreasonable bonus? Perhaps bonuses could be justified if they reflect a person's actual success in contributing to the profits of a company. This could be seen as an argument from desert or even as an argument from fair reciprocity. If an employee's actions have helped to bring about good economic outcomes, then it is appropriate that he or she receive a percentage of the company profits. If the economic outcomes have been bad, then no bonus is warranted. Nevertheless, what percentage is justified? Presumably this will depend on the number of other employees in the company and the level of contribution. That being said, it is tempting to think that a bonus should reflect not merely a person's actual success in contributing to the company's profits, but also his or her effort. After all, a person might have put in a great deal of effort but be working for an unsuccessful company. But this line of thought brings into view Rawls' point that even the willingness to make an effort is not purely the responsibility of the individual. Here we must consider the relative importance of deservingness, reciprocity and responsibility for effort.

Second, there is the question of government regulations to prevent irresponsible lending. The strange thing about the term 'irresponsible lending' is that in the absence of regulation it is not clear what it means. An often cited example is of mortgage companies offering to lend people as much as *six times* their salary. But if an applicant can afford the monthly repayments, why is it irresponsible? Part of the answer must be that it could have been reasonably foreseen by the banks that changes in interest rates or personal circumstances would make the mortgage unaffordable. Then again, buying a house with a mortgage will always carry some degree of risk. So if the buffer is too great, it effectively denies people a gamble they might want to take. Here the issue is how to strike a reasonable balance between paternalism and individual autonomy.

Third, there is the issue of how much emphasis to place on the detection and prosecution of tax evasion and white collar fraud. An appeal to the principle of treating like cases alike would imply that the state should spend at least as much money investigating these crimes as it does on detecting welfare fraud. But how much public money is it reasonable to devote to detecting and prosecuting these crimes given how difficult and expensive it can be to bring such cases to court? This question is motivated by recent high profile fraud trials in Britain which collapsed or the jury returned no verdict costing taxpayers tens of millions of pounds. The issue at stake here is whether or not to insist on the principle of treating like cases alike even in the face of legitimate concerns about the efficient use of public funds.

Finally, consider occurences of option luck. Recall from Chapter 3 that Dworkin characterises option luck as a matter of how deliberate and calculated gambles turn out. It is common for investors to be told that share prices can go down as well as up. If someone buys a share that goes down, then the option luck is bad. But is all option luck a matter of personal responsibility? Take the example of Icesave, part of the Icelandic bank Landsbanki, which collapsed in October 2008 leaving hundreds of thousands of depositors in Britain and other parts of Europe without access to their savings. The Labour government's response was to guarantee that no British Icesave customers would lose their savings, including those not covered by the standard Financial Services Compensation Scheme (FSCS) which protects up to £50,000 of savings. This was probably a wise move in the context of widespread financial uncertainty. In the words of Gordon Brown: 'We are showing by our actions that we stand by people who save in Britain.'[32] But is full compensation fair to other taxpayers?

Putting to one side local authorities who invested public money in Icesave, many private investors were attracted to its relatively high rates of interest and tax-free savings accounts. If Icesave had not collapsed, then these individuals would have expected to reap the rewards. So how can they now expect to avoid the losses? Why should other taxpayers be forced to compensate individuals who took a gamble and lost? This is, of course, a question of fairness. And we know that for some philosophers fairness is primarily about holding people responsible for deliberate gambles. But it seems to me that any plausible answer to this question is bound to depend to some extent on judgements of reasonableless: whether or not investors in Icesave could have reasonably predicted the bank's collapse; whether or not it is reasonable to allow someone to lose his or her entire life's savings because of one gamble. No doubt philosophy has something to add here. Nevertheless, I also think that the exploration of reasonableness in these cases would benefit from a wider public debate, meaning that politicians would do well to consult ordinary citizens as well as philosophers about whether or not it is reasonable to bail out savers and at what level.

In this chapter I have explored questions of personal responsibility in relation to rules dealing with unemployment benefits, the allocation of medical treatment, drug policy and regulations on personal debt and financial rewards. Liberal egalitarianism provides one possible framework for thinking about these issues. By focusing on fairness, however, this framework does not always capture other values that seem to be important here, such as human flourishing, autonomy, reasonableness and even compassion. But how are these different values to be weighed together? And how do we decide which policies are best all things considered? It is to these questions that I now turn.

8   So How Do We Decide?

The power of judging should not be given to a permanent senate but should be exercised by persons drawn from the body of the people at certain times of the year in the manner prescribed by law to form a tribunal which lasts only as long as necessity requires.

Charles de Montesquieu

When confronted with a set of moral values and principles some philosophers seek to develop rules that establish a fixed order of priority between them. My own view is that reasonable people can, and often do, disagree about priorities. To the lay person this view may seem like sitting on the fence. But I do not intend in this book to sit on the fence. Instead, I want to try to offer up a workable mechanism by which a set of priorities can be sought democratically. What can political representatives do to better engage with the views of philosophers and the general public on the right set of priorities? My argument will be that citizens' juries provide just such a method of deliberative engagement.

GETTING THE PUBLIC INVOLVED

The idea that there should be greater public involvement in decisions on social policy is by no means a new one. In 1968, for example, the Seebohm Report on social work optimistically declared that 'the development of citizen participation should reduce the rigid distinction between givers and takers of social services, and the stigma which being a client has involved in the past.'[1] More recently, Gordon Brown has used citizens' juries to help the government formulate policies, describing this as a 'politics of empowerment and engagement' and as something that 'embraces everyone in this nation'.[2]

That politicians wish to engage more with the public is perhaps not all that surprising. Some people regard this as a cynical ploy to abdicate responsibility for making tough, electorally risky decisions. Others prefer to see it as a genuine attempt to devolve political power, as a way of combating voter apathy and of injecting ideas into government from outside Westminster. I shall not rehearse the flaws of representative democracy here, suffice it to say that there are many of them and a large number have to do with misrepresentation of what 'the people' want, both majorities and minorities, lack of communication between politicians and voters, and some arrogance on the part of people in public office concerning the importance of accountability. In Brown's case, public consultation might be redemption for what happened in the run up to the Iraq war, when the Labour government was accused of being deaf to the wishes of the nation.

What is perhaps more surprising is that some philosophers actually advocate this strategy. In his book, *Welfare*, the American philosopher Nicholas Rescher explicitly comes out in favour of what he calls a 'democratic conception of the issue':

> In what respects and to what extent is *society*, working through the instrumentality of the state, responsible for the welfare of its members? What demands for the promotion of his welfare can an individual reasonably make upon his society? These are questions to which no answer can be sought in *a priori* reasoning alone. A complete answer depends not on a special realm of universal ultimates but *on what the society decides it should be*.[3]

I believe that there are a number of good reasons for getting the public involved in social policy decisions. One is to clarify

principles and values that can only be partially described by philosophers or only described in abstract terms. A related reason is
to judge the relative importance of these principles and values in
ways that might not be possible for philosophers working in isola-
tion and at the level of first principles.

A less philosophical, more political, reason for getting the
public involved is to improve trust between politicians and the
electorate in a time when there is a good deal of distrust and cyni-
cism about politicians and politics in general. Moreover, if citizens
have a strong sense that those in positions of power are willing
to take their views seriously on important policy issues, such
that they feel as though they are participants in a broader public
debate *with* politicians and policymakers, perhaps they will be
more willing to identify with and accept the resulting decisions,
including decisions which may highlight the need for greater
personal responsibility.

I also think there is an intrinsic connection between public
engagement and personal responsibility. Engagement in policy
decisions can be an example of personal responsibility as autonomy, since it affords citizens the chance to live in a society the
rights and responsibility of which they have been involved in
drawing up. This may not be the kind of individualistic autonomy
that comes when NHS patients are given the right to choose
which hospital to have their operations in. Nevertheless, it does
provide a kind of communal autonomy in which individuals
are able to deliberate about and form the rules of their society
together.

CITIZENS' JURIES

Rather than surveying every method of incorporating the views
of ordinary citizens into policy decisions – including referenda,
public consultation, community forums, focus groups, deliberative polls and citizens' juries – I intend to focus just on citizens'

juries. These build on the long tradition of juries within the legal system. This means that ordinary people already have an inkling of what they might involve. In the case of welfare reform the analogy to trial juries is even closer because sometimes the issue is whether or not economic sanctions (having benefits stopped) should be imposed.

In what follows I shall sketch out a role for citizens' juries in thinking about questions of personal responsibility as they pertain to various areas of social policy. I leave it to others to judge whether or not citizens' juries might also work well in other areas of government decision-making, such as the economy, foreign policy, law and order, public works and the environment.[4] But before describing the role that citizens' juries might play in social policy, I need first to make some general points.

A citizens' jury is a small-scale exercise of deliberative democracy in which a group of men and women, jurors, come together to find out more about an issue and try to bring their critical judgement and sense of reasonableness to bear upon that issue, hearing evidence, expressing their views, seeking common ground and drawing up recommendations. This is a deliberative exercise, meaning that jurors are there to deliberate with each other. It is also participatory rather than representative in the sense that citizens are there *in person*. Citizens' juries cannot claim moral authority from sheer weight of numbers or from being statistically representative of the population. What is special about citizens' juries, at least the juries I have in mind, is that they offer the chance for citizens to set the agenda for discussion, in contrast to top-down consultation exercises, and provide a truly public test of reasonableness. In large part, it is the quality of the deliberation that justifies the method. Even so, it is still important for the jurors to represent different groups in society and the conclusions they reach, which need not be unanimous, should be a fair reflection of the reasoning and values of the population as a whole.

The first British citizens' jury took place in March 1996. It focused on healthcare and was organised by the Institute for Public Policy Research (IPPR) in conjunction with Cambridge and Huntingdon Health Authority. The idea was later adopted by Gordon Brown and the first of his citizens' juries met in September 2007 at the Brunel Academy in Bristol. It concentrated on issues surrounding education and children's services. Along with his ministerial colleague Ed Balls, Brown was filmed talking with what appeared to be a diverse group of students, parents, teachers and community leaders. A film of the event was subsequently posted on the 10 Downing Street website.[5] The event was reported as costing in the region of £57,000 which compares favourably to the cost of a face-to-face opinion poll conducted by private pollsters such as Ipsos MORI. The cost of citizens' juries is significant because senior managers of healthcare trusts, for example, will find it difficult to justify spending large amounts of money on public consultation exercises when medical services are being cut.

Like other democratic procedures, the moral authority of the results will depend, in part, on the values of transparency and fairness. It didn't take long for Brown's citizens' juries to become embroiled in a row over fakery. In November 2007 the Conservatives seized upon evidence relating to the Bristol event which suggested that only 22 of the 38 people who attended were 'genuine' members of the public. The remaining participants were council staff or other officials drafted in to make the event a success. According to the Tories, the revelation proved that the entire project was a sham.[6] This conclusion seems to me to have been premature, however, given that subsequent citizens' juries, such as the jury on unpaid carers attended by Brown and Alan Johnson in Leeds in January 2008, avoided the same charges. The Leeds jury was not loaded with party members. On the contrary, the event was attended by 60 carers who discussed carers' benefits, improved access to social services and combining care with employment. This was part of a larger public consultation exercise which fed into the development of the government's 2008 National Strategy for Carers.[7]

In terms of fair representation, it is important that approximately equal numbers of men and women take part and that there is adequate representation of different socio-economic classes within society as well as of minority ethno-religious groups, people with disabilities, gays and lesbians and people from different age groups. Consequently, citizens' juries must be planned and executed in such as way as to enable recruitment from all sections of society. This could mean, for example, that expenses paid to jurors should be high enough to cover the cost of decent childcare and that juries should take place in locations that have proper access facilities. In their study of the IPPR pilot schemes, Anna Coote and Jo Lenaghan report that everyone was paid a flat rate of £200 for their time. They believed that 'it would be unfair to have significant wage differentials reflected within the jury'. But they also report no major difficulty in recruiting high earners onto the juries.[8]

Jurors should also be able to understand the material created by the commissioning body and to comprehend the information and arguments of expert witnesses. Responsibility will fall on witnesses to speak in plain English wherever possible, which also goes for any philosophers invited to the juries. Even so, one barrier to inclusion can be lack of basic literacy, numeracy and comprehension skills on the part of prospective jurors. Therefore additional support should be made available to people with learning difficulties so that they are not practically excluded from taking part.

In addition to this, every participant should have roughly the same chance to hear and discuss evidence, to question and interrogate, to set the terms and the procedures of the debate. One report describes how the moderator or facilitator of some citizens' juries encouraged jurors to establish their own rules of behaviour and reasoning for the jury.[9] I am not unsympathetic to this innovation, but I also believe that there is room for some general guidelines here. The academic literature on deliberative democracy is vast and there is a swelling sub-stream of work reflecting on how badly some theories of deliberative democracy cater to diversity and difference. The main thrust of this work is that norms of deliberation should not favour men over women and should not be culturally specific. This implies, for example, that citizens' juries should not privilege 'speech that is assertive and confrontational' over speech that is 'tentative, exploratory, or conciliatory'. They should permit expressions of 'anger, hurt, and passionate concern' as well as speech that is 'dispassionate'. It also implies that citizens' juries should be open not just to judgment, inference and evidence but also to 'greeting, rhetoric, and storytelling' and to 'figurative language'.[10]

Some citizens' juries have been more successful than others on this score. In 2006 the National Institute for Health and Clinical Excellence (NICE), a not-for-profit non-governmental organisation which provides national guidance on promoting good health, initiated a Citizens' Council made up of 30 ordinary members of the public, reflecting diversity in age, gender, socio-economic status and ethnicity. The Citizens' Council meets every so often to hear expert information on contentious topics surrounding medical need and healthcare provision, to thoroughly discuss the issues raised and to report its recommendations to NICE. Studies of the early life of the Council, however, indicate that the moments of genuine deliberation were few and far between. Studies also found that the white male majority was often the dominant voice and that there were tensions between the evidence-based discourse of professionals and the personal narratives of citizens.[11]

For these reasons it is judicious to lay down some basic ground rules for how citizens' juries should be conducted, which could be covered in a brief training session prior to the commencement of the jury. The rules might include how people may address one another and the witnesses and how much time should be given over for each juror to cross-examine witnesses and to have his or her say. The ground rules might also make it clear that a range of methods of deliberation are permitted. If jurors are taken from all walks of life, then inevitably they will include all kinds of people.

This is to be welcomed. Even so, people who bring to the juries hatred, prejudice and intolerance must operate within basic standards of public deliberation and human decency. Finally, the juries should be able to show how the decisions they have reached can be explained or justified by the evidence they have taken from witnesses and their own deliberations.

One additional defect shared by both the IPPR's pilot schemes and NICE's Citizens' Council is that the agendas were set in advance by the public authority which commissioned the jury. I don't deny the fact that *someone* has to set the agenda, otherwise public deliberation will descend into a free-for-all. But what I do wish to question is the appropriateness of the commissioning authority taking sole charge of setting the agenda. I propose instead a new model for citizens' juries in which both the commissioning authority and the jurors help to develop the agenda from the start. In practice, this might require a reasonably lengthy pre-jury exercise in which jurors are given a broad topic for the impending jury and asked to submit possible questions to be placed onto the agenda. Through a process of refinement and collaboration it may then be possible to arrive at an agreed agenda. Indeed, this pre-jury exercise may act as a useful screening process for identifying problems with the objectives of the jury or weaknesses in the questions to be discussed or even prejudicial jurors in advance of the actual jury.

In the past citizens' juries have been funded by the commissioning bodies, which in the case of juries looking into social policy issues will be local authorities, hospital trusts, government departments and non-governmental organisations and charities. This may not in itself be a problem save for the fact that since it is paying for the jury an authority might reasonably expect to set its own agenda. For this reason there may be a case for establishing an independent fund to which bodies can apply should they wish to run a jury. The authority in charge of the fund could then set out the guidelines for the juries and provide regulation. This has the merit of building a degree of independence and accountability. Being optimistic, there may be scope for conducting a series of juries around the country for any given social policy dilemma. What happens if different juries come up with different solutions? One solution is to bring the juries together in some sort of grand jury or citizens' summit. The various recommendations could then be developed into an aggregate answer.

As for the jurors themselves, I can see no reason why individual citizens shouldn't appear on consecutive juries, drawing on their experiences to help first-time jurors. I also think it is right that participating in a citizens' jury should be accepted by caseworkers as a 'good cause' for someone in receipt of Jobseeker's Allowance not attending an interview. There is even a case for including participation in citizens' juries, either as juror or witness, among the reasonable offers of work or civic labour that can be made to people under the New Deal. However, it would be wrong to fill the juries up with large numbers of welfare recipients as this could skew the results unfairly.

With these preliminaries out of the way, what role might citizens' juries play in thinking about personal responsibility? There are lots of possibilities. First, they could be asked to think about some of the different moral principles and values that are relevant to policy-making, such as those discussed in previous chapters of this book, including the proposed right to personal responsibility. Second, they could be asked to determine the exact boundaries of important moral distinctions, such as the distinction between choice and circumstance, and to weigh the relative importance of different values. Third, they could be asked to reflect on some specific policy dilemmas: to judge the merits of unconditional basic income and the level at which it might be set; to lay down conventions concerning the operation of social welfare programmes, such as by establishing a list of reasonable excuses for failing to attend interviews under the New Deal; to think about what constitutes an appropriate contribution to society in return for welfare benefits; to reflect on the principles of allocation for scarce medical resources; to think about the amount of money it is appropriate to spend on drug treatment programmes and acceptable levels of success; to consider new regulations for IVAs; to think about possible guidelines for the financial rewards and bonuses paid to talented high-flyers and company directors; to reflect on the relative importance of pursuing benefits cheats and white collar fraudsters. Finally, they could be asked to decide specific cases, such as Mr X, and to make decisions about the free provision of certain kinds of medicines and treatments within the NHS.

Certainly some of these roles will chime more naturally with people's preconceptions of what a jury does than others. Based on their assessment of citizens' juries Coote and Lenaghan conclude as follows: 'The jury model appears to be more appropriate for choosing between clearly-defined options or for developing guidelines for decision-makers, than for producing detailed plans or considering abstract ideas.'[12] This, I think, further underscores the need for a robust period of preparation before jurors even meet. Following the advice of Coote and Lenaghan, it may not be fruitful to ask jurors to consider moral principles and values in the abstract. It may be that they just won't have any firm intuitions one way or the other. Nevertheless, one solution to this problem is to provide jurors with concrete illustrations or case studies as a way of getting to grips with these principles and values. But which ones? Organisers could introduce examples from the philosophical literature or, better yet, invite philosophers to present these examples. To make sure that all bases are covered they could also offer up stories of ordinary people found in newspapers. In so far as reasonableness and human compassion call for face-to-face contact with human beings, there is also a case for asking real people to tell their stories to citizens' juries directly. Take the case of the Afghan poppy farmers who came to Britain in February of 2006 to meet British MPs and to speak directly with former heroin addicts through the Blackburn Citizens' Jury, for example.[13]

What kind of expert witnesses are appropriate? As the name suggests, an expert witness is someone with expertise that is relevant to the issue at hand. There may be little value in asking an expert on farming to attend a citizens' jury on drugs policy; unless, of course, he is an expert on poppy-seed production. However, it is also important to recognise that witnesses will not only provide answers to the problems, they will to some extent frame what the 'real' problems are. If the jury is interested in problem drug use, for example, an expert on medical health will probably frame the issue in terms of treating addiction, an expert in the field of child protection might look at the problem from the particular perspective of the impact of addiction on any children involved, and a social security expert may be especially exercised by the task of getting people off benefits and back into work. The upshot is that the selection of experts is not in itself a neutral decision.[14]

I think that this reinforces the importance of a sound pre-jury procedure in which jurors are able to identify whom *they* believe the relevant witnesses will be. This process should ensure that the juries receive evidence from a range of experts. Due to the nature of the issues, it is entirely appropriate for jurors to hear from politicians, policymakers, civil servants, front line workers, welfare recipients, the Citizens' Advice Bureau, independent think tanks, pressure groups, sociologists, opinion pollsters, economists, political scientists and philosophers. Indeed, philosophers have played an important role in countless Royal Commissions over the years and contribute to influential non-governmental bodies such as the Nuffield Council on Bioethics. Of course, if the commissioning authority does not have the sole prerogative to say who the relevant experts are, this raises the possibility of expert witnesses being called upon who are known to the general public for the radical solutions they offer to familiar social problems. The members of a citizens' jury might decide to call expert witnesses whose evidence directly challenges long-standing government policy. This is to be expected and is not unwelcome I think.

But what is the exact status of citizens' juries? Won't jury recommendations simply be ignored by commissioning authorities, meaning that they will become a sop to the public in return for public authorities pushing though controversial decisions? I concede this danger, but I also believe it will be reduced if juries are done well. Coote and Lenaghan counsel the following conditions for a successful citizens' jury. The commissioning body should have the power to act on the jury's recommendations and should make a firm commitment of time and attention to the jury and its conclusions. It should publicise the fact that a jury has been convened and the issues being addressed; publish the jury's recommendations; undertake to respond publicly within a given time frame; explain in public which recommendations it intends to act upon and how as well as being clear about which recommendations it intends to ignore and why.[15]

Does this mean that juries – or the public body which regulates the juries – should be given special powers or legal instruments to force commissioning bodies, including local authorities or even government departments, to enact their recommendations? I think that this would be both impracticable and undesirable. It might add yet another layer to the existing system of national government, regional government, mayoral government and local government. I propose instead that commissioning authorities should have statutory duties to adequately reflect upon the jury's recommendations and to respond publicly to them. Moreover, an independent ombudsman should be available in cases where the jury and the authority disagree over whether or not these statutory duties have been fulfilled in good faith.

In a representative democracy like Britain citizens cannot realistically expect representatives to give up ultimate control over decision-making on social policy. But this doesn't mean that the democratic system will be hopelessly compromised if citizens have a greater role in the public debate which feeds into such decision-making. Needless to say, the recommendations of citizens' juries will feed into political decisions along with various other inputs, including different forms of public consultation and, of course, the views of MPs, Lords, pressure groups, the media, business leaders, professional lobbyists, and so on. Moreover, politicians and policymakers will need to take account of various special considerations, not least department budgets, manifesto pledges, the economic cycle, national emergencies, the drive for re-election, international agreements on immigration and, of course, the Human Rights Act 1998. Assuming these factors counterbalance each other, politicians working in consultation with the public will have to steer a course between the extremes of too much or too little personal responsibility.

ANSWERING SOME POTENTIAL CRITICISMS

No democratic method is perfect and certainly not citizens' juries. One potential criticism concerns the role of juries in thinking about very complex issues. In a time when some experts on the criminal justice system are questioning the appropriateness of using juries for complex fraud cases, why bring them in here? Among the reasons given for getting rid of trial by jury in fraud cases are that they are typically very lengthy and costly. Another reason is that due to the intricacy of the evidence judges are often compelled to limit indictments in order to make the arguments comprehensible for juries. Making cases more manageable comes at the cost of justice. It is worth keeping in mind, however, that unlike juries in the criminal justice system, citizens' juries meet for a prescribed period of time, which is normally a matter of days. No doubt there is a balancing act to be made between providing jurors with all the relevant evidence, no matter how complex, and not overwhelming them with unmanageable streams of information. But there is perhaps not quite the same demand to pull on every single thread. The jurors can appropriately leave some of the finer details to be worked out by policymakers further downstream.

A second criticism concerns participation. In chapter 5 I suggested that rather than conceiving citizens as passive bearers of a set of rights and responsibilities handed down to them by the state, citizens should be seen as agents who participate in decisions about rights and responsibilities. But what if citizens simply don't wish to participate in the juries? My proposal initially is that governments should encourage participation, not that it should be compulsory. The juries will be made up of volunteers from the general population, where a lottery process could be used to select the final participants in the event that a jury is inundated with applicants. That said, there may be scope in time to bring citizens' juries in line with the rules on jury service used in the criminal justice system. In Britain anyone on the electoral register aged between 18 and 70 can be called for jury service. Home Office research from 1999 estimates that two-thirds of people called for jury service are granted excusal not to appear, such as people with medical conditions, people caring for young children or elderly relatives, and people with pre-booked holidays.[16] Similar rules could apply to citizens' juries. But whereas judges, police officers, ministers of religion, MPs, soldiers and members of the medical profession are all exempt from jury service, there is every reason to include such people in citizens' juries, either as jurors or as witnesses.

A final criticism has to do with the suitability of certain jurors. Some people might see it as inappropriate to consult welfare recipients about the future direction of social policy. Under the Poor Laws recipients of poor relief were not entitled to vote. Being in receipt of poor relief was viewed as incompatible with claiming any democratic rights. By analogy, how can it be right to allow people to serve on citizens' juries – a weighty social responsibility – if they have previously shown no inclination to work for a living or fulfil the reciprocal burdens of citizenship in some other way? Nevertheless, I believe there are two good reasons to adopt a more progressive attitude. First, it is important that all sections of society, or as many as possible, are represented. The fairness of the recommendations given will depend, in part, on composition. Second, if people have previously shown no inclination to accept the burdens of citizenship, then arguably this is all the more reason to encourage them to do so in the future, to be more responsible citizens.

In this chapter I have defended citizens' juries as my indirect 'answer' to the various questions of personal responsibility posed in this book.

9 Conclusion

It is never easy to sum up the reflections of an entire book, especially when so much ground has been covered. But I shall nevertheless try to highlight some of the main conclusions.

The central thrust of my argument is that personal responsibility matters from an ethical perspective and it does so for a number of different reasons. The many reasons discussed in this book were fairness, utility, self-respect, autonomy, human flourishing, natural duty and special obligation. Given this plurality of reasons, selecting a suitable regime of personal responsibility throws up some interesting policy dilemmas.

One such dilemma is that if we value personal responsibility not simply for reasons of fairness but also for reasons of autonomy and human flourishing, in some cases we have reason not to hold individuals responsible for the adverse consequences of their past choices, so that they might be better able to assume personal responsibility later on. One justification for funding drug treatment programmes, for example, is to rehabilitate people's capacity for responsible agency. Of course, some people may insist that fairness is the dominant value here and therefore should take priority. If upholding fairness means enforcing consequential responsibility on individuals at certain times by withholding assistance, then so be it. I have not attempted to settle this dispute here. Instead, I have proposed a mechanism by which public authorities can listen to the views of ordinary people concerning how to prioritise the different values and principles in play.

I have assumed that if a society extols personal responsibility as a moral good, then it is not unfitting for its elected officials to try to promote personal responsibility as a moral good. Perhaps some readers will be alarmed by the perfectionist overtones of this argument. But the argument is offered with the following caveat. Although I do not think it incumbent upon the state to refrain entirely from espousing views about the good life, I do think that the state must provide room for a vigorous and inclusive public debate about which conception of the good life to promote. More importantly, that debate must include a serious discussion about the relative importance of different values. There may be many occasions when it is legitimate to give priority to fairness over considerations of the good life.

Another implication of my argument is that there should be a right to personal responsibility, meaning that it is appropriate to spend taxpayers' money on giving positive encouragement and practical support to people to take greater personal responsibility for their own lives. This can be done in different ways. Sanctions are by their nature punitive, but a great many other state interventions are not. In the genre of unemployment, caseworkers can use their influence over welfare recipients to persuade them to seek work, the government can provide training, subsidised travel, free childcare, working tax credits, can pay financial incentives to employers to take on unemployed people and can even become an employer of last resort.

Perhaps some will say that cajoling people into work and smoothing the way with public funds is self-defeating because personal responsibility is about acting on one's own initiative and being self-reliant. I think this challenge deserves to be taken seriously, but I also think it can be answered. Suppose we accept that in an ideal world everyone would assume personal responsibility for their own lives, in the right ways and at the right times without the intervention of the state. It does not follow from this that lesser degrees of personal responsibility are worthless. As a society we might value spontaneous acts of personal responsibility above acts of personal responsibility that depend on state intervention or bribery. Even so, holding this view about the relative merits of different kinds of personal responsibility is perfectly consistent with believing that all acts of personal responsibility can be valuable to some degree.

Before a government takes any steps to promote personal responsibility, however, it must first consider whether the ends justify the means. One desideratum is that society places sufficiently high value upon personal responsibility to warrant the relevant intervention and, moreover, that there are no alternative policies which could yield the same results with lesser or cheaper intervention. A second desideratum is that any proposed means for promoting personal responsibility must not be self-defeating, as in, undermine the values they seek to promote. The example of compulsory medical insurance autonomy illustrates the problem. Compulsory insurance can work to protect people's long-term capacity for autonomy. As noted in previous chapters, however, some people object to compulsory insurance schemes on the grounds that they are paternalistic and deny autonomy. I take this problem seriously and I do not think there can be a blanket justification for compulsory insurance. The argument for such insurance must fight its corner against legitimate objections.

In Chapter 8 I defended citizens' juries as one promising way of incorporating the views of ordinary people as well as philosophers into social policy decisions. The model I proposed was one of jurors being involved in setting the agenda; having the opportunity to hear evidence from and scrutinise various expert witnesses, including philosophers, whom they can call and interrogate themselves; being able to reflect and deliberate freely and equally with each other on a set of issues which they may narrow down or broaden out as they wish; having the chance to make formal recommendations at the end. The overall aim should be to bring perspectives into areas of public policy that have hitherto seen little or no public involvement. To borrow the words of the American philosopher John Roemer: 'I do not have a theory which would enable me to discover exactly what aspects of a person's environment are beyond his control and affect his relevant behaviour in a way that relieves him or her of personal accountability for that behaviour. In actual practice, the society in question shall decide, through some political process, what it wishes to deem "circumstances".[1]

Notes

Chapter 1

1. See Robert Nozick (1974) *Anarchy, State, and Utopia*, Oxford: Blackwell, John Rawls (1971) *A Theory of Justice*, Oxford: Oxford University Press, Ronald Dworkin (1981a) 'What is Equality? Part 1: Equality of Welfare', *Philosophy and Public Affairs* 10, 185–246, (1981b) 'What is Equality? Part 2: Equality of Resources', *Philosophy and Public Affairs* 10, 283–345, (2000) *Sovereign Virtue*, Cambridge, MA: Harvard University Press, and (2006) *Is Democracy Possible Here?*, Princeton, NJ: Princeton University Press.

2. See respectively Gerald Gaus (2000) *Political Concepts and Political Theories*, Boulder, CO: Westview Press, Raymond Geuss (2008) *Philosophy and Real Politics*, Princeton, NJ: Princeton University Press and Jonathan Wolff (2006) *Introduction to Political Philosophy (Second Edition)*, Oxford: Oxford University Press.

3. Work and Pensions Select Committee (2007a) *Benefits Simplification: Volume I, Seventh Report of Session 2006–07*, available at www.publications.parliament.uk/pa/cm200607/cmselect/cmworpen/463/463i.pdf, paragraphs 28–31.

4. See David Cameron (2007a) Speech at Base 33, 16 February, available at www.base33.org.uk/C2B/PressOffice/display.asp?ID=32&Type=2, (2007b) Interview with the Today Programme, 23 April, available at http://news.bbc.co.uk/1/hi/uk_politics/6584123.stm, (2007c) Speech to the Conservative Party conference, 3 October, available at www.conservatives.com/tile.do?def=news.story.page&obj_id=139453&speeches=1, (2008a) Speech at the Glasgow East by-election campaign, 7 July, available at www.telegraph.co.uk/

news/newstopics/politics/conservative/2263705/David-Cameron-attacks-UK-%27moral-neutrality%27---full-text.html?pageNum=1, (2008b) Speech to the Conservative Party conference, 1 October, available at http://news.bbc.co.uk/1/hi/uk_politics/7646660.stm, and (2008c) 'There Are 5 Million People On Benefits In Britain: How Do We Stop Them Turning Into Karen Matthews?', *Mail Online*, 8 December, available at www.dailymail.co.uk/news/article-1092588/DAVID-CAMERON-There-5-million-people-benefits-Britain-How-stop-turning-this.html.

Chapter 2

1. For more on personal responsibility and externalities, see David Schmidtz (1998) 'Taking Responsibility' in D. Schmidtz and R. Goodin (eds) *Social Welfare and Individual Responsibility*, Cambridge: Cambridge University Press, p. 8.
2. Galen Strawson (1998) 'Free Will' in E. Craig (ed.) *Routledge Encyclopedia of Philosophy*, London: Routledge.
3. Dworkin (2000) p. 287.
4. For further discussion of these issues, see Julian Le Grand (1991) *Equity and Choice*, London: HarperCollins, pp. 97–100 and Richard Arneson (2001) 'Luck and Equality: Part II', *Proceedings of the Aristotelian Society*, supp. vol. 75, 73–90, pp. 85–6.
5. H. L. A. Hart (1968) *Punishment and Responsibility*, Oxford: Oxford University Press, pp. 212–13.
6. Thomas Scanlon (1998) *What We Owe to Each Other*, Cambridge, MA: Harvard University Press, p. 292.
7. Dworkin (2000) p. 490 n.9.
8. For more on the concept of welfare, see James Griffin (1986) *Well-Being*, Oxford: Clarendon Press and Tania Burchardt (2005) 'Just Happiness?' in N. Pearce and W. Paxton (eds) *Social Justice: Building a Fairer Britain*, London: IPPR.
9. Dworkin (1981a) p. 229.
10. Richard Arneson (1989) 'Equality and Equal Opportunity for Welfare', *Philosophical Studies* 56, 77–93, p. 88.
11. BBC News Online (2006b) 'Make People Happier, Says Cameron', 22 May, available at http://news.bbc.co.uk/1/hi/uk_politics/5003314.stm.

12. John Rawls (1996) *Political Liberalism*, New York: (
    Press, p. 189.
13. See Amartya Sen (1980) 'Equality of What?' in S
    Lectures on Human Values: Volume I, Salt Lake City
    Press and (1985) *Commodities and Capabilities*, /
    Holland.

Chapter 3

1. Hart (1968) pp. 149–52, 227–8.
2. See John Rawls (1982) 'Social Unity and Primary Goods' in A. Sen and B. Williams (eds) *Utilitarianism and Beyond*, Cambridge: Cambridge University Press, pp. 168–9, (1985) 'Justice as Fairness: Political not Metaphysical', *Philosophy and Public Affairs* 14, 223–51, p. 234, (2001) *Justice as Fairness: A Restatement*, Cambridge, MA: Harvard University Press, p. 45 and Arthur Ripstein (1999) *Equality, Responsibility, and the Law*, Cambridge: Cambridge University Press, p. 272.
3. G. A. Cohen (1989) 'On the Currency of Egalitarian Justice', *Ethics* 99, 906–44, p. 922. See also Arneson (1989) p. 86 and Le Grand (1991) pp. 86–7.
4. See Richard Arneson (1997) 'Postscript to Equality and Equal Opportunity for Welfare' in L. Pojman and R. Westmoreland (eds) *Equality*, New York: Oxford University Press, p. 239 and (2000a) 'Welfare Should Be the Currency of Justice', *Canadian Journal of Philosophy* 30, 497–524, p. 507.
5. G. A. Cohen (1993) 'Equality of What? On Welfare, Goods, and Capabilities' in M. Nussbaum and A. Sen (eds) *The Quality of Life*, Oxford: Oxford University Press, p. 28.
6. Hart (1968) p. 29.
7. Dworkin (2000) pp. 6, 294.
8. Ibid., p. 323.
9. Ibid., p. 287.
10. Dworkin (1981b) p. 293.
11. See Susan Hurley (2003) *Justice, Luck, and Knowledge*, Cambridge, MA: Harvard University Press, ch. 6.
12. Elizabeth Anderson (1999a) 'What is the Point of Equality?', *Ethics* 109, 287–337.

Samuel Scheffler (2005) 'Choice, Circumstance, and the Value of Equality', *Politics, Philosophy and Economics* 4, 5–28, p. 15.

14. See Carl Knight (2005) 'In Defence of Luck Egalitarianism', *Res Publica* 11, 55–73, Alexander Brown (2005) 'Luck Egalitarianism *and* Democratic Equality', *Ethical Perspectives* 12, 293–339 and Ronald Dworkin (2003) 'Equality, Luck and Hierarchy', *Philosophy and Public Affairs* 31, 190–8.

15. Harry Frankfurt (1971) 'Freedom of the Will and the Concept of a Person', *Journal of Philosophy* 68, 5–22.

16. See Dworkin (1981b) pp. 302–3 and (2000) pp. 290–5.

17. Cohen (1989) p. 923 and (2004) 'Expensive Tastes Rides Again' in J. Burley (ed.) *Dworkin and His Critics*, Malden, MA: Blackwell, p. 11.

18. See Dworkin (2000) ch. 7 and (2004) 'Ronald Dworkin Replies' in J. Burley (ed.) *Dworkin and His Critics*, Malden, MA: Blackwell.

19. See Cohen (1989) p. 921 and Le Grand (1991) p. 87.

20. Arneson (1989) pp. 85–8.

21. Compare Bhikhu Parekh (2006) *Rethinking Multiculturalism: Cultural Diversity and Political Theory (Second Edition)*, Houndsmill: Palgrave Macmillan, p. 151 and Brian Barry (2001) *Culture and Equality*, Cambridge: Polity, p. 37.

22. See Anderson (1999a) pp. 288–9 and Dworkin (2000) p. 321.

23. Charles Murray (1984) *Losing Ground*, New York: Basic Books, pp. 197–9.

24. Richard Arneson (1999a) 'Egalitarianism and Responsibility', *Journal of Ethics* 3, 225–47, pp. 238–41.

25. George Sher (1987) *Desert*, Princeton, NJ: Princeton University Press, p. 46.

26. Amartya Sen (1999) *Development as Freedom*, Oxford: Oxford University Press, p. 8.

27. See, for example, Scanlon (1998) ch. 6.

28. Anderson (1999a) pp. 322–4.

29. Stuart White (2003) *The Civic Minimum: On the Rights and Obligations of Economic Citizenship*, Oxford: Oxford University Press.

30. A. M. Buyx (2008) 'Personal Responsibility for Health as a Rationing Criterion: Why We Don't Like It and Why Maybe We Should', *Journal of Medical Ethics* 34, 871–4.

31. See Hillel Steiner (1994) *An Essay on Rights*, Oxford: Blackwell and

(1998) 'Choice and Circumstance' in A. Mason (ed.) *Ideals of Equality*, Oxford: Blackwell, pp. 99–100 n.12.

32. Eric Rakowski (1991) *Equal Justice*, Oxford: Clarendon Press, p. 153.

33. Cohen (1989) p. 934.

34. Dworkin (1981b) and (2000) ch. 9.

35. D. Halpern *et al.* (2004) *Personal Responsibility and Changing Behaviour*, Prime Minister's Strategy Unit, Cabinet Office, February, available at www.cabinetoffice.gov.uk/media/cabinetoffice/strategy/assets/pr2.pdf, p. 11.

36. Cohen (1989) p. 934.

Chapter 4

1. See Jeremy Bentham (2007) *Introduction to Principles of Morals and Legislation [1789]*, Mineola, NY: Dover.

2. For more on utilitarian analysis in public policy, see Daniel Hausman and Michael McPherson (2006) *Economic Analysis, Moral Philosophy, and Public Policy*, Cambridge: Cambridge University Press.

3. For a seminal philosophical account of the concept of self-respect, see Stephen Darwall (1977) 'Two Kinds of Respect', *Ethics* 88, 36–49.

4. Rawls (1971) p. 440.

5. Rawls (1996) p. lix.

6. Katherine Newman (1999) *No Shame in My Game: The Working Poor in the Inner City*, New York: Knopf.

7. See Jonathan Wolff (1998) 'Fairness, Respect, and the Egalitarian Ethos', *Philosophy and Public Affairs* 27, 97–122, Timothy Hinton (2001) 'Must Egalitarians Choose Between Fairness and Respect?', *Philosophy and Public Affairs* 30, 72–87 and Catriona McKinnon (2003) 'Basic Income, Self-respect and Reciprocity', *Journal of Applied Philosophy* 20, 143–58.

8. Bruce Landesman (1983) 'Egalitarianism', *Canadian Journal of Philosophy* 13, 27–56, pp. 36–7.

9. See H. T. Engelhardt Jr (1996) *The Foundations of Bioethics (Second Edition)*, New York, Oxford: Oxford University Press.

10. Sher (1987) p. 40.

11. See Hart (1968) pp. 45–7 and Scanlon (1998) pp. 251–3.

12. Reverend Thomas R. Malthus (1992) *An Essay on the Principle of Population [1798]*, Cambridge: Cambridge University Press, p. 101.

13. J. A. Hobson (1996) *The Social Problem [1902]*, Bristol: Thoemmes Press, p. 121.

14. See Karl Marx (1975) *Economic and Philosophical Manuscripts [1844]* in L. Colletti (ed.) *Karl Marx Early Writings*, Harmondsworth: Penguin, pp. 326–9, (1976) *Capital, Vol. 1 [1867]*, Ben Fowkes (trans.), Harmondsworth: Penguin, pp. 163–77 and Sean Sayers (1988) *Marxism and Human Nature*, London: Routledge.

15. See Eva Feder Kittay (1997) 'Human Dependency and Rawlsian Equality' in D. T. Meyers (ed.) *Feminists Rethink the Self*, Boulder, CO: Westview Press and (2005) 'Dependency, Difference, and Global Ethic of Longterm Care', *The Journal of Political Philosophy* 13, 443–69.

16. See John Locke (1988) *Two Treatises of Government [1689]*, Cambridge: Cambridge University Press, p. 291 and (1993) *John Locke Political Writings*, Harmondsworth: Penguin, pp. 440, 452.

17. See Will Kymlicka (1989) 'Liberal Individualism and Liberal Neutrality', *Ethics* 99, 883–905 and Rawls (1996).

18. Richard Arneson (1999b) 'Equality of Opportunity for Welfare Defended and Recanted', *The Journal of Political Philosophy* 7, 488–97, p. 497 and (2000b) 'Luck Egalitarianism and Prioritarianism', *Ethics* 110, 339–49, p. 343.

19. Wolff (1998) p. 122.

Chapter 5

1. Cameron (2008b) Speech to the Conservative Party conference.

2. Social Justice Policy Group (2007) *Breakthrough Britain: Ending the Costs of Social Breakdown*, available at www.centreforsocialjustice. org.uk/default.asp?pageRef=226.

3. Cameron (2008a) Speech at the Glasgow East by-election campaign.

4. See, for example, Murray (1984) p. 180.

5. Robert Rector (1997) 'Wisconsin's Welfare Miracle: How It Cut Its Caseload In Half', *Policy Review* 82, March and April, available at www.hoover.org/publications/policyreview/3573807.html.

6. Cameron (2007c) Speech to the Conservative Party conference.

7. Salvation Army (2004) *The Responsibility Gap: Individualism, Community and Responsibility in Britain Today*, London: The Henley Centre, available at www1.salvationarmy.org.uk/uki/www_uki. nsf/0/4D65410FC9F673D980256F970054526D/$file/Library-ResponsibilityGap.pdf.

8. Barack Obama (2008a) Speech to the Annual Convention of the NAACP, Cincinnati, Ohio, 14 July, available at www.usatoday.com/news/politics/election2008/2008-07-14-obama-naacp_N.htm.

9. Barack Obama (2008b) Speech to the Democratic National Convention, Denver, Illinois, 28 August, available at www.demconvention.com/barack-obama/.

10. Information gathered from the Basic Income Earth Network, available at www.basicincome.org/bien/, the US Basic Income Guarantee Network, www.usbig.net/, Basic Income Studies, available at www.bepress.com/bis/ and Citizen's Income Online, available at www.citizensincome.org.

11. Frank Field (1998) *New Ambitions for Our Country: A New Contract for Welfare*, London: HMSO, p. 80.

12. Gordon Brown (1998) Interview with Mary Riddell, *Daily Mail*, 1 August.

13. Alistair Darling (2001) Speech delivered to the Institute for Public Policy Research (IPPR) conference, 4 July, available at www.ippr.org.uk/research/files/team23/project28/Darling4.07.01.doc.

14. HM Government (2007a) *In Work, Better Off: Next Steps to Full Employment*, Norwich: HMSO, available at www.dwp.gov.uk/welfarereform/in-work-better-off/in-work-better-off.pdf.

15. HM Government (2007b) *Welfare Reform Act 2007*, available at www.opsi.gov.uk/acts/acts2007/pdf/ukpga_20070005_en.pdf.

16. David Freud (2007) *Reducing Dependency, Increasing Opportunity: Options for the Future of Welfare to Work*, Norwich: HMSO.

17. Cited in Work and Pensions Select Committee (2007b) *Full Employment and World Class Skills: Responding to the Challenges, Eighth Report of Session 2006–07*, available at www.publications.parliament.uk/pa/cm200607/cmselect/cmworpen/939/939.pdf.

18. Gordon Brown (2008b) Interview with Jon Sopel, 25 January, available at http://news.bbc.co.uk/1/hi/programmes/politics_show/7202283.stm.

19. Gordon Brown (2008d) Prime Minister's foreword to *Fair Rules for*

Strong Communities, London: HM Government, available at www.communities.gov.uk/documents/corporate/pdf/1083358.pdf, p. 4.

20. House of Commons (2009) *Welfare Reform Bill*, available at www.publications.parliament.uk/pa/cm200809/cmbills/067/09067.i-iii.html.

21. BBC News Online (2008c) '"Work for Benefits" Plan Unveiled', 21 July, available at http://news.bbc.co.uk/1/hi/uk_politics/7516551.stm.

22. Cameron (2008b) Speech to the Conservative Party conference.

23. Steve Webb (2009) 'Government Masks the Real Problems in the Welfare System', 11 March, available at www.libdems.org.uk/home/welfare-reform-bill-2008-09-189468140;show.

24. BBC News Online (2008a) 'Purnell Heads Reshuffle Changes', 24 January, available at http://news.bbc.co.uk/1/hi/uk_politics/7207497.stm.

25. HM Government (2007c) *Disability Equality Impact Assessment: Pathways to Work Rollout and Incapacity Benefits Reform*, 9 May, available at www.dwp.gov.uk/welfarereform/docs/DEIA.pdf.

26. BBC News Online (2008b) '"Work or Lose Home" Says Minister', 5 February, available at http://news.bbc.co.uk/1/hi/uk/7227667.stm.

27. James Purnell (2009) Speech to the House of Commons, 23 January, available at www.dwp.gov.uk/aboutus/2009/23-01-09.asp.

28. Ed Miliband (2005) 'Does Inequality Matter?' in A. Giddens and P. Diamond (eds) *The New Egalitarianism*, Cambridge: Polity, p. 49.

29. See Anderson (1999a) p. 316 and (1999b) 'Symposium on Anderson: Reply', *Brown Electronic Article Review Service (BEARS)* 22, December, available at www.brown.edu/Departments/Philosophy/bears/homepage.html.

30. BBC News Online (2006a) 'Cameron Vows to Defend "Free" NHS', 4 January, available at http://news.bbc.co.uk/1/hi/uk_politics/4578440.stm.

31. BBC News Online (2008d) '"Distressing" top-ups ban lifted', 5 November, available at http://news.bbc.co.uk/1/hi/health/7706921.stm.

32. US Census Bureau (2007) *Income, Poverty, and Health Insurance Coverage in the United States*, available at www.census.gov/prod/2007pubs/p60-233.pdf.

33. Barack Obama and John McCain (2008) Third presidential debate, Hofstra University, New York, 15 October.

34. For an overview of these studies, see David Brown (2008) 'In the Balance: Some Candidates Disagree, But Studies Show It's Often Cheaper To Let People Get Sick', *Washington Post*, 8 April, available at www.washingtonpost.com.

35. Gordon Brown (2008a) Speech at King's College London, 7 January, available at www.politics.co.uk/news/opinion-former-index/health/gordon-brown-on-nhs-$483887.htm.

36. The draft constitution and consultation documents are available at www.dh.gov.uk/en/Publicationsandstatistics/Publications/PublicationsPolicyAndGuidance/DH_085814.

37. Andrew Lansley (2008) Speech to the think tank Reform, 27 August, available at www.guardian.co.uk/commentisfree/2008/aug/27/health.nhs.

38. Tony Blair (2006) 'No More Coded Critiques – Let's Have an Open Debate on Where We Go Next', *Guardian*, 27 June, available at www.guardian.co.uk/commentisfree/2006/jun/27/comment.politics.

39. David Cameron (2006) Speech at the launch of the Young Adult Trust, 30 October, available at www.guardian.co.uk/politics/2006/oct/30/conservatives.voluntarysector.

40. Quoted in Will Woodward (2006) 'Cameron Promises UK Bill of Rights to Replace Human Rights Act', *Guardian*, 26 June, available at www.guardian.co.uk/politics/2006/jun/26/uk.humanrights.

41. Gordon Brown (2007a) Leadership launch speech, 11 May, available at http://news.bbc.co.uk/1/hi/uk_politics/6644717.stm.

42. See House of Commons Joint Committee on Human Rights (2008) *A Bill of Rights for the UK? Twenty-ninth Report of Session 2007–08*, London: The Stationery Office Limited, available at www.publications.parliament.uk/pa/jt200708/jtselect/jtrights/165/165i.pdf and Yvonne Denier (2005) 'On Personal Responsibility and the Human Right to Healthcare', *Cambridge Quarterly of Healthcare Ethics* 14, 224–34.

43. See Wesley Newcomb Hohfeld (1946) *Fundamental Legal Conceptions as Applied in Judicial Reasoning*, New Haven, CT: Yale University Press and Murray Rothbard (1982) 'Law, Property Rights and Air Pollution', *Cato Journal* 2, 55–99.

44. Gordon Brown (2000) Speech at the National Council for Voluntary Organisations (NCVO) annual conference, 9 February, available at www.hm-treasury.gov.uk/newsroom_and_speeches/speeches/chancellorexchequer/speech_chex_90200.cfm.

45. Quoted in David Goodhart (2004) 'Discomfort of Strangers', *Guardian*, 24 February, p. 24.

46. David Miller (2006) 'Multiculturalism and the Welfare State: Theoretical Reflections' in K. Banting and W. Kymlicka (eds) *Multiculturalism and the Welfare State: Recognition and Redistribution in Advanced Democracies*, Oxford: Oxford University Press.

47. Gordon Brown (2006b) Speech to the Labour Party conference, 25 September, available at www.guardian.co.uk/politics/2006/sep/25/labourconference.labour2.

48. 50 Gordon Brown (2006a) Speech at the Fabian New Year conference, 14 January, available at www.fabians.org.uk/events/new-year-conference-06/brown-britishness/speech.

49. Brown (2006b) Speech to the Labour Party conference.

50. See, for example, David Goodhart (2005) 'Britain's Glue: The Case for Liberal Nationalism' in A. Giddens and P. Diamond (eds) *The New Egalitarianism*, Cambridge: Polity.

51. For a more general discussion of the problem of multiple nationalities, see Will Kymlicka (1995) *Multicultural Citizenship*, Oxford: Clarendon Press.

52. See, for example, Catherine Needham (2003) *Citizen-Consumers: New Labour's Marketplace Democracy, Catalyst Working Paper*, available at www.editiondesign.com/catalyst/pubs/pub10.html.

53. Joint Committee on Human Rights (2008) p. 6.

54. Cameron (2008b) Speech to the Conservative Party conference.

55. Cameron (2008a) Speech at the Glasgow East by-election campaign.

56. House of Commons Committee of Public Accounts (2008) *Tax Credits and PAYE, Eighth Report of Session 2007–08*, London: The Stationery Office Limited, available at www.parliament.the-stationery-office.com/pa/cm200708/cmselect/cmpubacc/300/30002.htm.

57. Sarah Womack (2007) 'Brown Urged to Reform UK Welfare Policy', 6 November, available at www.telegraph.co.uk/news/newstopics/politics/labour/1568349/Brown-urged-to-reform-UK-welfare-policy.html.

58. David Cameron (2009) Speech on the economy, London, 5 January, available at http://news.bbc.co.uk/1/hi/uk_politics/7810932.stm.

Chapter 6

1. Tom Sefton (2003) 'What We Want from the Welfare State' in A. Park *et al. British Social Attitudes: 20th Report*, London: Sage, p. 7.
2. Peter Taylor-Gooby (2004) 'The Work-Centred Welfare State' in A. Park *et al. British Social Attitudes: 21st Report*, London: Sage, p. 13.
3. Andrew Levine (1998) *Rethinking Liberal Equality*, Ithaca, NY: Cornell University Press.
4. See Peter Dwyer (2000) *Welfare Rights and Responsibilities*, Bristol: The Policy Press, (2002) 'Making Sense of Social Citizenship', *Critical Social Policy* 22, 273–99, (2004) *Understanding Social Citizenship*, Cambridge: Policy Press and Steffen Mau (2004) 'Welfare Regimes and the Norms of Reciprocal Exchange', *Current Sociology* 52, 53–74.
5. Jonathan Wolff (2000) 'Beyond Responsibility', *Times Literary Supplement*, 5 May, pp. 28–9.
6. Sefton (2003) p. 16.
7. Peter Taylor-Gooby and Rose Martin (2008) 'Trends in Sympathy for the Poor' in E. Clery *et al. British Social Attitudes: the 24th Report*, London: Sage, p. 237.
8. Taylor-Gooby (2004) p. 8.
9. Sefton (2003) p. 17.
10. Taylor-Gooby (2004) p. 8.
11. Tom Sefton (2005) 'Give and Take: Public Attitudes to Redistribution' in A. Park *et al. British Social Attitudes: 22nd Report*, London: Sage, p. 26.
12. Taylor-Gooby (2004) p. 8.
13. David Miller (2005) 'What is Social Justice?' in N. Pearce and W. Paxton (eds) *Social Justice: Building a Fairer Britain*, London: IPPR, pp. 5, 18.
14. Peter Taylor-Gooby (2005) 'Attitudes to Social Welfare' in N. Pearce and W. Paxton (eds) *Social Justice: Building a Fairer Britain*, London: IPPR.
15. Sefton (2005) p. 26.
16. Peter Taylor-Gooby and Charlotte Hastie (2002) 'Support for State Spending: Has New Labour Got it Right?' in A. Park *et al. British Social Attitudes: 19th Report*, London: Sage, p. 87.
17. See Alan Hedges (2005) *Perceptions of Redistribution: Report on Exploratory Qualitative Research*, London: London School of

Economics, available at http://sticerd.lse.ac.uk/dps/case/cp/CASEpaper96.pdf.

18. John Hills (2003) 'Inclusion or Insurance? National Insurance and the Future of the Contributory Principle', Centre for Analysis of Social Exclusion, London School of Economics, available at http://sticerd.lse.ac.uk/dps/case/cp/CASEpaper68.pdf.

19. Polly Toynbee and David Walker (2008) *Unjust Rewards: Exposing Greed and Inequality in Britain Today*, London: Granta Books, p. 25.

20. Ibid., p. 34.

21. OECD (2008) *Employment Outlook*, Paris: OECD, pp. 360–6.

22. See P. van Baal *et al.* (2008) 'Lifetime Medical Costs of Obesity: Prevention No Cure for Increasing Health Expenditure', *Public Library of Science Medicine* 5, e29.

23. Cited in Halpern *et al.* (2004) p. 13.

24. R. Boarini *et al.* (2006) 'Moral Intuitions About Social Inequalities and Individual Responsibility: A European Comparison', *Human Development and Capability Association*, 28 August, available at www.capabilityapproach.com/pubs/2_5_Boarini.pdf.

25. Jonathan Wolff and Avner de-Shalit (2007) *Disadvantage*, Oxford: Oxford University Press, p. 37.

26. See Martha Nussbaum (2000) *Women and Human Development: The Capabilities Approach*, Cambridge: Cambridge University Press and Wolff and de-Shalit (2007) p. 106.

27. Rawls (1971) pp. 48–50.

Chapter 7

1. In the three months to January 2009, unemployment in Britain grew to 2.03 million people, 6.5 per cent of the working population. The number of people receiving Jobseeker's Allowance was 1.39 million, meaning fierce competition for vacancies advertised in Jobcentres. Office for National Statistics (2009) *Labour Market Statistics March 2009*, available at www.statistics.gov.uk/pdfdir/lmsuk0309.pdf. In the US, the number of unemployed persons increased to 13.2 million in March 2009, representing 8.5 per cent of the working population. Bureau of Labor Statistics (2009) Employment Situation Summary, 3 April, available at www.bls.gov/news.release/empsit.nr0.htm.

2. Lawrence Mead (1997) 'From Welfare to Work' in A. Deacon (ed.) *From Welfare to Work*, London: Institute of Economic Ideas Health and Welfare Unit, p. 20.

3. Lawrence Mead (1986) *Beyond Entitlement*, New York: Free Press.

4. Commission on Social Justice (1994) *Social Justice*, London: Institute for Public Policy Research, p. 239.

5. Some studies suggest that the success of such schemes depends on the professionalism of the caseworkers as well as an ethos of 'help and hassle'. See Eithne McLaughlin (1994) 'Workfare – a Pull, a Push, or a Shove?' in A. Deacon (ed.) *From Welfare to Work*, London: Institute of Economic Ideas Health and Welfare Unit and Mary Bane and David Ellwood (1994) *Welfare Realities*, Cambridge, MA: Harvard University Press.

6. See Dworkin (2000) p. 336 and Paul Bou-Habib and Serena Olsaretti (2004) 'Liberal Egalitarianism and Workfare', *Journal of Applied Philosophy* 21, 257–70.

7. Dwyer (2000) pp. 146–53.

8. Commission on Social Justice (1994) p. 239.

9. Quoted in Daniel Moynihan (1996) 'Congress Builds a Coffin', *New York Review of Books* 43, 11 January, 33–6.

10. See Bandana Ahmad (1992) *Black Perspectives in Social Work*, Birmingham: Venture Press, Fiona Williams (1988) *Social Policy: A Critical Introduction*, Cambridge: Polity and Robert Drake (2001) *The Principles of Social Policy*, Basingstoke: Palgrave Macmillan.

11. Regulation 73(2)(b) of the Jobseeker's Allowance Regulations 1996.

12. E. A. L. Bano (2002) *Decision R(JSA) 7/03*, 30 September, available at www.osscsc.gov.uk/judgmentfiles/j900/R(JSA)%207-03%20bv%20final.doc.

13. Le Grand (1991) p. 105.

14. General Medical Council (2006) *Good Medical Practice*, 13 November, available at www.gmc-uk.org/guidance/good_medical_practice/index.asp.

15. Roger Dobson (2008) 'Obesity Does Not Limit Benefits of Knee Replacement, Study Shows', *British Medical Journal* 337, a1061.

16. For an interesting discussion of priority setting in Swedish cardiac care, see L. Ridderstolpe *et al.* (2003) 'Priority Setting in Cardiac Surgery: A Survey of Decision Making and Ethical Issues', *Journal of Medical Ethics* 29, 353–8.

17. Harald Schmidt (2007) 'Patients' Charters and Health Responsibilities', *British Medical Journal* 335, 1187–9.

18. See Home Office Research, Development and Statistics Directorate (2002) *Home Office Research Study 249: The Economic and Social Costs of Class A Drug Use in England and Wales, 2000*, available at www. homeoffice.gov.uk/rds/pdfs2/hors249.pdf, (2007) *Online Report 21/07: Local and National Estimates of the Prevalence of Opiate Use and/or Crack Cocaine Use (2004/05)*, available at www.homeoffice. gov.uk/rds/pdfs07/rdsolr2107.pdf and Martin Frischer *et al.* (2001) 'A Comparison of Different Methods for Estimating the Prevalence of Problematic Drug Misuse in Great Britain', *Addiction*, 96, 1465–76.

19. HM Treasury (2004) *Spending Review: Public Service Agreements 2005–2008, 21: Action Against Illegal Drugs*, available at www.hm-treasury. gov.uk/media/F/2/sr04_psa_ch21.pdf.

20. Home Office (2008) *Drugs: Protecting Families and Communities: The 2008 Drug Strategy*, available at http://drugs.homeoffice.gov.uk/ drug-strategy/overview/, p. 32.

21. Elizabeth Stewart (2007) 'Figures Reveal High Cost of "Curing" Drug Addicts', *Guardian*, 30 October, available at www.guardian.co.uk/ politics/2007/oct/30/immigrationpolicy.drugsandalcohol.

22. Arthur Gould and Nina Stratford (2002) 'Illegal Drugs: Highs and Lows' in A. Park *et al. British Social Attitudes: 19th Report*, London: Sage.

23. Credit Action (2009) *Debt Statistics January 2009*, available at www.creditaction.org.uk/debt-statistics.html.

24. Ibid.

25. Jill Treanor and Rupert Jones (2007) 'Banks Shoot Down IVA Rockets', *Guardian*, 30 January, available at www.guardian.co.uk/money/2007/ jan/30/creditanddebt.business.

26. Anthony Giddens (1994) *Beyond Left and Right: The Future of Radical Politics*, Cambridge: Polity, (1998) *The Third Way: The Renewal of Social Democracy*, Cambridge: Polity and (2000) *The Third Way and its Critics*, Cambridge: Polity.

27. Gordon Brown (2008c) Speech to the United Nations in New York, 26 September.

28. Rawls (1971) p. 74.

29. David Miller (1999) *Principles of Social Justice*, Cambridge, MA: Harvard University Press, p. 68.

30. For this line of argument, see G. A. Cohen (2000) *If You're an Egalitarian, How Come You're So Rich?*, Cambridge, MA: Harvard University Press.

31. See Robert Peston (2008) *Who Runs Britain? How Britain's New Elite Are Changing Our Lives*, London: Hodder and Stoughton.

32. Independent (2008) 'Brown Hails "Bold" £50bn Rescue', 8 October, available at www.independent.co.uk/news/uk/politics/brown-hails-bold--pound50bn-rescue-954754.html.

Chapter 8

1. Committee on Local Authority and Allied Personal Social Services (1968) *Report*, London: HMSO, para. 492.

2. Gordon Brown (2007b) Speech to the National Council for Voluntary Organisations, 3 September, available at www.number10.gov.uk/output/Page13008.asp.

3. Nicholas Rescher (1972) *Welfare*, Pittsburgh: University of Pittsburgh Press, p. 114.

4. See, for example, Ian Shapiro (1999) *Democratic Justice*, New Haven, CT: Yale University Press.

5. Available at www.number10.gov.uk/output/page13091.asp.

6. Jane Merrick (2007) 'Brown's Landmark Citizens' Juries Scheme in Fakery Row', *Daily Mail*, 16 November, available at www.dailymail.co.uk/pages/live/articles/news/news.html?in_article_id=494548&in_page_id=1770&ito=1490.

7. HM Government (2008) *Carers at the Heart of 21st Century Families and Communities: A Caring System on Your Side, A Life of Your Own*, 10 June, available at www.dh.gov.uk/en/Publicationsandstatistics/Publications/PublicationsPolicyAndGuidance/DH_085345.

8. Anna Coote and Jo Lenaghan (1997) *Citizens' Juries: From Theory to Practice*, London: IPPR, p. 72.

9. Clare Delap (1998) *Making Better Decisions: Report of an IPPR Symposium on Citizens' Juries and Other Methods of Public Involvement*, London: IPPR, p. 13.

10. See, for example, Iris Marion Young (1996) 'Communication and the Other: Beyond Deliberative Democracy' in S. Benhabib (ed.) *Democracy and Difference: Contesting the Boundaries of the Political*,

Princeton, NJ: Princeton University Press, pp. 123–5. For further discussion, see Melissa Williams (2000) 'The Uneasy Alliance of Group Representation and Deliberative Democracy' in W. Kymlicka and W. Norman (eds) *Citizenship in Diverse Societies*, Oxford: Oxford University Press.

11. C. Davies *et al.* (2006) *Citizens at the Centre: Deliberative Participation in Healthcare Decisions*, Bristol: The Policy Press.

12. Coote and Lenaghan (1997) p. v.

13. Senlis Council (2006) 'Landmark Journey of Afghan Farmers to the United Kingdom', February, available at www.senliscouncil.net/ modules/events/london_farmers.

14. H. K. Colebatch (2002) *Policy (Second Edition)*, Buckingham: Open University Press, p. 29.

15. Coote and Lenaghan (1997) p. 68.

16. Home Office Research, Development and Statistics Directorate (1999) *Research Findings No 102: Jury Excusal and Deferral*, available at www.homeoffice.gov.uk/rds/pdfs/r102.pdf.

Chapter 9

1. John Roemer (1998) *Equality of Opportunity*, Cambridge, MA: Harvard University Press, p. 8.

Bibliography

Aesop (1996) *Aesop's Fables [circa 6th century BC]*, Harmondsworth: Penguin.

Ahmad, B. (1992) *Black Perspectives in Social Work*, Birmingham: Venture Press.

Anderson, E. (1999a) 'What is the Point of Equality?', *Ethics* 109, 287–337.

— (1999b) 'Symposium on Anderson: Reply', *Brown Electronic Article Review Service (BEARS)* 22, December, available at www.brown.edu/Departments/Philosophy/bears/homepage.html.

Aristotle (2004) *The Nicomachean Ethics [circa 350 BC]*, J. A. K. Thomson (trans.), Harmondsworth: Penguin.

Arneson, R. (1989) 'Equality and Equal Opportunity for Welfare', *Philosophical Studies* 56, 77–93.

— (1997) 'Postscript to Equality and Equal Opportunity for Welfare' in L. Pojman and R. Westmoreland (eds) *Equality*, New York: Oxford University Press.

— (1999a) 'Egalitarianism and Responsibility', *Journal of Ethics* 3, 225–47.

— (1999b) 'Equality of Opportunity for Welfare Defended and Recanted', *The Journal of Political Philosophy* 7, 488–97.

— (2000a) 'Welfare Should Be the Currency of Justice', *Canadian Journal of Philosophy* 30, 497–524.

— (2000b) 'Luck Egalitarianism and Prioritarianism', *Ethics* 110, 339–49.

— (2001) 'Luck and Equality: Part II', *Proceedings of the Aristotelian Society*, supp. vol. 75, 73–90.

Bane, M. and Ellwood, D. (1994) *Welfare Realities*, Cambridge, MA: Harvard University Press.

Bano, E. A. L. (2002) *Decision R(JSA) 7/03*, 30 September, available at www.osscsc.gov.uk/judgmentfiles/j900/R(JSA)%207-03%20bv%20final.doc.

Barry, B. (2001) *Culture and Equality*, Cambridge: Polity.

Bartholomew, J. (2006) *The Welfare State We're In (Second Edition)*, London: Politicos.

BBC News Online (2006a) 'Cameron Vows to Defend "Free" NHS', 4 January, available at http://news.bbc.co.uk/1/hi/uk_politics/4578440.stm.

— (2006b) 'Make People Happier, Says Cameron', 22 May, available at http://news.bbc.co.uk/1/hi/uk_politics/5003314.stm.

— (2007) 'Parents' Views on Benefits Reforms', 5 March, available at http://news.bbc.co.uk/1/hi/uk/6419447.stm.

— (2008a) 'Purnell Heads Reshuffle Changes', 24 January, available at http://news.bbc.co.uk/1/hi/uk_politics/7207497.stm.

— (2008b) '"Work or Lose Home" Says Minister', 5 February, available at http://news.bbc.co.uk/1/hi/uk/7227667.stm.

— (2008c) '"Work for Benefits" Plan Unveiled', 21 July, available at http://news.bbc.co.uk/1/hi/uk_politics/7516551.stm.

— (2008d) '"Distressing" top-ups ban lifted', 5 November, available at http://news.bbc.co.uk/1/hi/health/7706921.stm.

Benhabib, S. (ed.) (1996) *Democracy and Difference: Contesting the Boundaries of the Political*, Princeton, NJ: Princeton University Press.

Bentham, J. (2007) *Introduction to Principles of Morals and Legislation [1789]*, Mineola, NY: Dover.

— (1796) *Essays Relative to the Subject of the Poor Laws*, The Manuscripts of Jeremy Bentham, The Library of University College London, 152a.62.

Blair, T. (2001) Foreword to D. Blunkett (ed.) *Towards Full Employment in a Modern Society*, Norwich: HMSO.

— (2006) 'No More Coded Critiques – Let's Have an Open Debate on Where We Go Next', *Guardian*, 27 June, available at www.guardian.co.uk/commentisfree/2006/jun/27/comment.politics.

Boarini, R. *et al.* (2006) 'Moral Intuitions About Social Inequalities and Individual Responsibility: A European Comparison', *Human Development and Capability Association*, 28 August, available at www.capabilityapproach.com/pubs/2_5_Boarini.pdf.

Bou-Habib, P. and Olsaretti, S. (2004) 'Liberal Egalitarianism and Workfare', *Journal of Applied Philosophy* 21, 257–70.

Brown, A. (2005) 'Luck Egalitarianism *and* Democratic Equality', *Ethical Perspectives* 12, 293–339.

Brown, D. (2008) 'In the Balance: Some Candidates Disagree, But Studies Show It's Often Cheaper To Let People Get Sick', *Washington Post*, 8 April, available at www.washingtonpost.com.

Brown, G. (1998) Interview with Mary Riddell, *Daily Mail*, 1 August.

— (2000) Speech at the National Council for Voluntary Organisations (NCVO) annual conference, 9 February, available at www.hm-treasury. gov.uk/newsroom_and_speeches/speeches/chancellorexchequer/ speech_chex_90200.cfm.

— (2006a) Speech at the Fabian New Year conference, 14 January, available at www.fabians.org.uk/events/new-year-conference-06/brown- britishness/speech.

— (2006b) Speech to the Labour Party conference, 25 September, available at www.guardian.co.uk/politics/2006/sep/25/labourconference. labour2.

— (2007a) Leadership launch speech, 11 May, available at http://news. bbc.co.uk/1/hi/uk_politics/6644717.stm.

— (2007b) Speech to the National Council for Voluntary Organisations, 3 September, available at www.number10.gov.uk/output/Page13008. asp.

— (2008a) Speech at King's College London, 7 January, available at www. politics.co.uk/news/opinion-former-index/health/gordon-brown-on- nhs-$483887.htm.

— (2008b) Interview with Jon Sopel, 25 January, available at http://news. bbc.co.uk/1/hi/programmes/politics_show/7202283.stm.

— (2008c) Speech to the United Nations in New York, 26 September.

— (2008d) Prime Minister's foreword to *Fair Rules for Strong Communities*, London: HM Government, available at www.communities.gov.uk/ documents/corporate/pdf/1083358.pdf.

Burchardt, T. (2005) 'Just Happiness?' in N. Pearce and W. Paxton (eds) *Social Justice: Building a Fairer Britain*, London: IPPR.

Bureau of Labor Statistics (2009) *Employment Situation Summary*, 3 April, available at www.bls.gov/news.release/empsit.nr0.htm.

Buyx, A. M. (2008) 'Personal Responsibility for Health as a Rationing Criterion: Why We Don't Like It and Why Maybe We Should', *Journal of Medical Ethics* 34, 871–4.

Cameron, D. (2006) Speech at the launch of the Young Adult Trust, 30 October, available at www.guardian.co.uk/politics/2006/oct/30/ conservatives.voluntarysector.

— (2007a) Speech at Base 33, 16 February, available at www.base33.org. uk/C2B/PressOffice/display.asp?ID=32&Type=2.

— (2007b) Interview with the Today Programme, 23 April, available at http://news.bbc.co.uk/1/hi/uk_politics/6584123.stm.

— (2007c) Speech to the Conservative Party conference, 3 October, available at www.conservatives.com/tile.do?def=news.story.page&obj_id=139453&speeches=1.

— (2008a) Speech at the Glasgow East by-election campaign, 7 July, available at www.telegraph.co.uk/news/newstopics/politics/conservative/2263705/David-Cameron-attacks-UK-%27moral-neutrality%27---full-text.html?pageNum=1.

— (2008b) Speech to the Conservative Party conference, 1 October, available at http://news.bbc.co.uk/1/hi/uk_politics/7646660.stm.

— (2008c) 'There Are 5 Million People On Benefits In Britain: How Do We Stop Them Turning Into Karen Matthews?', *Mail Online*, 8 December, available at www.dailymail.co.uk/news/article-1092588/DAVID-CAMERON-There-5-million-people-benefits-Britain-How-stop-turning-this.html.

— (2009) Speech on the economy, London, 5 January, available at http://news.bbc.co.uk/1/hi/uk_politics/7810932.stm.

Cohen, G. A. (1989) 'On the Currency of Egalitarian Justice', *Ethics* 99, 906–44.

— (1993) 'Equality of What? On Welfare, Goods, and Capabilities' in M. Nussbaum and A. Sen (eds) *The Quality of Life*, Oxford: Oxford University Press.

— (2000) *If You're an Egalitarian, How Come You're So Rich?*, Cambridge, MA: Harvard University Press.

— (2003) 'Facts and Principles', *Philosophy and Public Affairs* 31, 211–45.

— (2004) 'Expensive Tastes Rides Again' in J. Burley (ed.) *Dworkin and His Critics*, Malden, MA: Blackwell.

Colebatch, H. K. (2002) *Policy (Second Edition)*, Buckingham: Open University Press.

Commission on Social Justice (1994) *Social Justice*, London: Institute for Public Policy Research.

Committee on Local Authority and Allied Personal Social Services (1968) *Report*, London: HMSO.

Coote, A. and Lenaghan, J. (1997) *Citizens' Juries: From Theory to Practice*, London: IPPR.

Credit Action (2009) *Debt Statistics January 2009*, available at www. creditaction.org.uk/debt-statistics.html.

Darling, A. (2001) Speech delivered to the Institute for Public Policy Research (IPPR) conference, 4 July, available at www.ippr.org.uk/ research/files/team23/project28/Darling4.07.01.doc.

Darwall, S. (1977) 'Two Kinds of Respect', *Ethics* 88, 36–49.

Davies, C. *et al.* (2006) *Citizens at the Centre: Deliberative Participation in Healthcare Decisions*, Bristol: The Policy Press.

Delap, C. (1998) *Making Better Decisions: Report of an IPPR Symposium on Citizens' Juries and Other Methods of Public Involvement*, London: IPPR.

Denier, Y. (2005) 'On Personal Responsibility and the Human Right to Healthcare', *Cambridge Quarterly of Healthcare Ethics* 14, 224–34.

Dobson, R. (2008) 'Obesity Does Not Limit Benefits of Knee Replacement, Study Shows', *British Medical Journal* 337, a1061.

Drake, R. (2001) *The Principles of Social Policy*, Basingstoke: Palgrave Macmillan.

Dworkin, R. (1981a) 'What is Equality? Part 1: Equality of Welfare', *Philosophy and Public Affairs* 10, 185–246.

— (1981b) 'What is Equality? Part 2: Equality of Resources', *Philosophy and Public Affairs* 10, 283–345.

— (2000) *Sovereign Virtue*, Cambridge, MA: Harvard University Press.

— (2003) 'Equality, Luck and Hierarchy', *Philosophy and Public Affairs* 31, 190–8.

— (2004) 'Ronald Dworkin Replies' in J. Burley (ed.) *Dworkin and His Critics*, Malden, MA: Blackwell.

— (2006) *Is Democracy Possible Here?*, Princeton, NJ: Princeton University Press.

Dwyer, P. (2000) *Welfare Rights and Responsibilities*, Bristol: The Policy Press.

— (2002) 'Making Sense of Social Citizenship', *Critical Social Policy* 22, 273–99.

— (2004) *Understanding Social Citizenship*, Cambridge: Policy Press.

Engelhardt Jr, H. T. (1996) *The Foundations of Bioethics (Second Edition)*, New York, Oxford: Oxford University Press.

Feder Kittay, E. (1997) 'Human Dependency and Rawlsian Equality' in D. T. Meyers (ed.) *Feminists Rethink the Self*, Boulder, CO: Westview Press.

— (2005) 'Dependency, Difference, and Global Ethic of Longterm Care', *The Journal of Political Philosophy* 13, 443–69.

Field, F. (1998) *New Ambitions for Our Country: A New Contract for Welfare*, London: HMSO.

Frankfurt, H. (1971) 'Freedom of the Will and the Concept of a Person', *Journal of Philosophy* 68, 5–22.

Freud, D. (2007) *Reducing Dependency, Increasing Opportunity: Options for the Future of Welfare to Work*, Norwich: HMSO.

Frischer, M. *et al.* (2001) 'A Comparison of Different Methods for Estimating the Prevalence of Problematic Drug Misuse in Great Britain', *Addiction*, 96, 1465–76.

Gaus, G. (2000) *Political Concepts and Political Theories*, Boulder, CO: Westview Press.

General Medical Council (2006) *Good Medical Practice*, 13 November, available at www.gmc-uk.org/guidance/good_medical_practice/index.asp.

Geuss, R. (2008) *Philosophy and Real Politics*, Princeton, NJ: Princeton University Press.

Giddens, A. (1994) *Beyond Left and Right: The Future of Radical Politics*, Cambridge: Polity.

— (1998) *The Third Way: The Renewal of Social Democracy*, Cambridge: Polity.

— (2000) *The Third Way and its Critics*, Cambridge: Polity.

Goodhart, D. (2004) 'Discomfort of Strangers', *Guardian*, 24 February.

— (2005) 'Britain's Glue: The Case for Liberal Nationalism' in A. Giddens and P. Diamond (eds) *The New Egalitarianism*, Cambridge: Polity.

Goodin, R. (1995) *Utilitarianism as a Public Philosophy*, Cambridge: Cambridge University Press.

— (1998a) *Reasons for Welfare*, Princeton, NJ: Princeton University Press.

— (1998b) 'Social Welfare as a Collective Consequential Responsibility' in D. Schmidtz and R. Goodin (eds) *Social Welfare and Individual Responsibility*, Cambridge: Cambridge University Press.

Gould, A. and Stratford, N. (2002) 'Illegal Drugs: Highs and Lows' in A. Park *et al. British Social Attitudes:19th Report*, London: Sage.

Griffin, J. (1986) *Well-Being*, Oxford: Clarendon Press.

Halpern, D. *et al.* (2004) *Personal Responsibility and Changing Behaviour*, Prime Minister's Strategy Unit, Cabinet Office, February, available at www.cabinetoffice.gov.uk/media/cabinetoffice/strategy/assets/pr2.pdf.

Hart, H. L. A. (1968) *Punishment and Responsibility*, Oxford: Oxford University Press.

Hausman, D. and McPherson, M. (2006) *Economic Analysis, Moral Philosophy, and Public Policy*, Cambridge: Cambridge University Press.

Hedges, A. (2005) *Perceptions of Redistribution: Report on Exploratory Qualitative Research*, London: London School of Economics, available at http://sticerd.lse.ac.uk/dps/case/cp/CASEpaper96.pdf.

Hills, J. (2003) 'Inclusion or Insurance? National Insurance and the Future of the Contributory Principle', Centre for Analysis of Social Exclusion, London School of Economics, available at http://sticerd.lse.ac.uk/dps/case/cp/CASEpaper68.pdf.

Hinton, T. (2001) 'Must Egalitarians Choose Between Fairness and Respect?', *Philosophy and Public Affairs* 30, 72–87.

HM Government (2007a) *In Work, Better Off: Next Steps to Full Employment*, Norwich: HMSO, available at www.dwp.gov.uk/welfarereform/in-work-better-off/in-work-better-off.pdf.

— (2007b) *Welfare Reform Act 2007*, available at www.opsi.gov.uk/acts/acts2007/pdf/ukpga_20070005_en.pdf.

— (2007c) *Disability Equality Impact Assessment: Pathways to Work Rollout and Incapacity Benefits Reform*, 9 May, available at www.dwp.gov.uk/welfarereform/docs/DEIA.pdf.

— (2008) *Carers at the Heart of 21st Century Families and Communities: A Caring System on Your Side, A Life of Your Own*, 10 June, available at www.dh.gov.uk/en/Publicationsandstatistics/Publications/PublicationsPolicyAndGuidance/DH_085345.

HM Treasury (2004) *Spending Review: Public Service Agreements 2005–2008, 21: Action Against Illegal Drugs*, available at www.hm-treasury.gov.uk/media/F/2/sr04_psa_ch21.pdf.

Hobson, J. A. (1996) *The Social Problem [1902]*, Bristol: Thoemmes Press.

Hohfeld, W. N. (1946) *Fundamental Legal Conceptions as Applied in Judicial Reasoning*, New Haven, CT: Yale University Press.

Home Office (2007) *Drugs: Our Community, Your Say: The 2007 Drug Strategy Consultation*, available at http://drugs.homeoffice.gov.uk/publication-search/drug-strategy/drug-strategy-consultation.pdf?view=Binary.

— (2008) *Drugs: Protecting Families and Communities: The 2008 Drug Strategy*, available at http://drugs.homeoffice.gov.uk/drug-strategy/overview/.

Home Office Research, Development and Statistics Directorate (1999) *Research Findings No. 102: Jury Excusal and Deferral*, available at www.homeoffice.gov.uk/rds/pdfs/r102.pdf.

— (2002) *Home Office Research Study 249: The Economic and Social Costs of Class A Drug Use in England and Wales, 2000*, available at www.homeoffice.gov.uk/rds/pdfs2/hors249.pdf.

— (2007) *Online Report 21/07: Local and National Estimates of the Prevalence of Opiate Use and/or Crack Cocaine Use (2004/05)*, available at www.homeoffice.gov.uk/rds/pdfs07/rdsolr2107.pdf.

House of Commons (2009) *Welfare Reform Bill*, available at www.publications.parliament.uk/pa/cm200809/cmbills/067/09067.i-iii.html.

House of Commons Committee of Public Accounts (2008) *Tax Credits and PAYE, Eighth Report of Session 2007–08*, London: The Stationery Office Limited, available at www.parliament.the-stationery-office.com/pa/cm200708/cmselect/cmpubacc/300/30002.htm.

House of Commons Joint Committee on Human Rights (2008) *A Bill of Rights for the UK? Twenty-ninth Report of Session 2007–08*, London: The Stationery Office Limited, available at www.publications.parliament.uk/pa/jt200708/jtselect/jtrights/165/165i.pdf.

Hurley, S. (2003) *Justice, Luck, and Knowledge*, Cambridge, MA: Harvard University Press.

Independent (2008) 'Brown Hails "Bold" £50bn Rescue', 8 October, available at www.independent.co.uk/news/uk/politics/brown-hails-bold--pound50bn-rescue-954754.html.

Knight, C. (2005) 'In Defence of Luck Egalitarianism', *Res Publica* 11, 55–73.

Kymlicka, W. (1989) 'Liberal Individualism and Liberal Neutrality', *Ethics* 99, 883–905. — (1995) *Multicultural Citizenship*, Oxford: Clarendon Press.

— (2002) *Contemporary Political Philosophy (Second Edition)*, Oxford: Oxford University Press.

Landesman, B. (1983) 'Egalitarianism', *Canadian Journal of Philosophy* 13, 27–56.

Lansley, A. (2008) Speech to the think tank Reform, 27 August, available at www.guardian.co.uk/commentisfree/2008/aug/27/health.nhs.

Le Grand, J. (1991) *Equity and Choice*, London: HarperCollins.

— (2006) *Motivation, Agency and Public Policy: Of Knights and Knaves, Pawns and Queens*, Oxford: Oxford University Press.

Levine, A. (1998) *Rethinking Liberal Equality*, Ithaca, NY: Cornell University Press.

Locke, J. (1988) *Two Treatises of Government [1689]*, Cambridge: Cambridge University Press.

— (1993) *John Locke Political Writings*, Harmondsworth: Penguin.

McKinnon, C. (2003) 'Basic Income, Self-respect and Reciprocity', *Journal of Applied Philosophy* 20, 143–58.

McLaughlin, E. (1994) 'Workfare – a Pull, a Push, or a Shove?' in A. Deacon (ed.) *From Welfare to Work*, London: Institute of Economic Ideas Health and Welfare Unit.

Malthus, Rev. T. R. (1992) *An Essay on the Principle of Population [1798]*, Cambridge: Cambridge University Press.

Marshall, T. H. (1963) *Citizenship and Social Class [1950]* in his *Sociology at the Crossroads*, London: Heinemann.

Marx, K. (1975) *Economic and Philosophical Manuscripts [1844]* in L. Colletti (ed.) *Karl Marx Early Writings*, Harmondsworth: Penguin.

— (1976) *Capital, Vol. 1 [1867]*, Ben Fowkes (trans.), Harmondsworth: Penguin.

Mau, S. (2004) 'Welfare Regimes and the Norms of Reciprocal Exchange', *Current Sociology* 52, 53–74.

Mead, L. (1986) *Beyond Entitlement*, New York: Free Press.

— (1997) 'From Welfare to Work' in A. Deacon (ed.) *From Welfare to Work*, London: Institute of Economic Ideas Health and Welfare Unit.

Merrick, J. (2007) 'Brown's Landmark Citizens' Juries Scheme in Fakery Row', *Daily Mail*, 16 November, available at www.dailymail.co.uk/pages/live/articles/news/news.html?in_article_id=494548&in_page_id=1770&ito=1490.

Miliband, E. (2005) 'Does Inequality Matter?' in A. Giddens and P. Diamond (eds) *The New Egalitarianism*, Cambridge: Polity.

Mill, J. S. (1972) *On Liberty [1859]* in *Utilitarianism, On Liberty, Considerations on Representative Government*, London: Everyman.

Miller, D. (1999) *Principles of Social Justice*, Cambridge, MA: Harvard University Press. — (2005) 'What is Social Justice?' in N. Pearce and W. Paxton (eds) *Social Justice: Building a Fairer Britain*, London: IPPR.

— (2006) 'Multiculturalism and the Welfare State: Theoretical Reflections' in K. Banting and W. Kymlicka (eds) *Multiculturalism and the Welfare State: Recognition and Redistribution in Advanced Democracies*, Oxford: Oxford University Press.

de Montesquieu, C. (1989) *The Spirit of the Laws [1748]*, Cambridge: Cambridge University Press.

Moynihan, D. (1996) 'Congress Builds a Coffin', *New York Review of Books* 43, 11 January.

Murray, C. (1984) *Losing Ground*, New York: Basic Books.

Needham, C. (2003) *Citizen-Consumers: New Labour's Marketplace Democracy, Catalyst Working Paper*, available at www.editiondesign.com/catalyst/pubs/pub10.html.

Newman, K. (1999) *No Shame in My Game: The Working Poor in the Inner City*, New York: Knopf.

Nozick, R. (1974) *Anarchy, State, and Utopia*, Oxford: Blackwell.

Nussbaum, M. (2000) *Women and Human Development: The Capabilities Approach*, Cambridge: Cambridge University Press.

Obama, B. (2008a) Speech to the Annual Convention of the NAACP, Cincinnati, Ohio, 14 July, available at www.usatoday.com/news/politics/election2008/2008-07-14-obama-naacp_N.htm.

— (2008b) Speech to the Democratic National Convention, Denver, Illinois, 28 August, available at www.demconvention.com/barack-obama/.

Obama, B. and McCain, J. (2008) Third presidential debate, Hofstra University, New York, 15 October.

OECD (2008) *Employment Outlook*, Paris: OECD.

Office for National Statistics (2009) *Labour Market Statistics March 2009*, available at www.statistics.gov.uk/pdfdir/lmsuk0309.pdf.

Parekh, B. (2006) *Rethinking Multiculturalism: Cultural Diversity and Political Theory (Second Edition)*, Houndmills: Palgrave Macmillan.

Peston, R. (2008) *Who Runs Britain? How Britain's New Elite Are Changing Our Lives*, London: Hodder and Stoughton.

Phillips, A. (1995) *The Politics of Presence*, Oxford: Oxford University Press.

Purnell, J. (2009) Speech to the House of Commons, 23 January, available at www.dwp.gov.uk/aboutus/2009/23-01-09.asp.

Rakowski, E. (1991) *Equal Justice*, Oxford: Clarendon Press.

Rawls, J. (1971) *A Theory of Justice*, Oxford: Oxford University Press.

— (1982) 'Social Unity and Primary Goods' in A. Sen and B. Williams (eds) *Utilitarianism and Beyond*, Cambridge: Cambridge University Press.

— (1985) 'Justice as Fairness: Political not Metaphysical', *Philosophy and Public Affairs* 14, 223–51.

— (1996) *Political Liberalism*, New York: Columbia University Press.

— (2001) *Justice as Fairness: A Restatement*, Cambridge, MA: Harvard University Press.

Rector, R. (1997) 'Wisconsin's Welfare Miracle: How It Cut Its Caseload In Half', *Policy Review* 82, March and April, available at www.hoover.org/publications/policyreview/3573807.html.

Rescher, N. (1972) *Welfare*, Pittsburgh: University of Pittsburgh Press.

Ridderstolpe, L. *et al.* (2003) 'Priority Setting in Cardiac Surgery: A Survey of Decision Making and Ethical Issues', *Journal of Medical Ethics* 29, 353–8.

Ripstein, A. (1999) *Equality, Responsibility, and the Law*, Cambridge: Cambridge University Press.

Roemer, J. (1998) *Equality of Opportunity*, Cambridge, MA: Harvard University Press.

Rothbard, M. (1982) 'Law, Property Rights and Air Pollution', *Cato Journal* 2, 55–99.

Salvation Army (2004) *The Responsibility Gap: Individualism, Community and Responsibility in Britain Today*, London: The Henley Centre, available at www1.salvationarmy.org.uk/uki/www_uki.nsf/0/4D65410FC9F673D980256F970054526D/$file/Library-ResponsibilityGap.pdf.

Sayers, S. (1988) *Marxism and Human Nature*, London: Routledge.

Scanlon, T. (1998) *What We Owe to Each Other*, Cambridge, MA: Harvard University Press.

Scheffler, S. (2005) 'Choice, Circumstance, and the Value of Equality', *Politics, Philosophy and Economics* 4, 5–28.

Schmidt, H. (2007) 'Patients' Charters and Health Responsibilities', *British Medical Journal* 335, 1187–9.

Schmidtz, D. (1998) 'Taking Responsibility' in D. Schmidtz and R. Goodin (eds) *Social Welfare and Individual Responsibility*, Cambridge: Cambridge University Press.

Sefton, T. (2003) 'What We Want from the Welfare State' in A. Park *et al. British Social Attitudes: 20th Report*, London: Sage.

— (2005) 'Give and Take: Public Attitudes to Redistribution' in A. Park *et al. British Social Attitudes: 22nd Report*, London: Sage.

Sen, A. (1980) 'Equality of What?' in S. M. McMurrin (ed.) *Lectures on Human Values: Volume I*, Salt Lake City: University of Utah Press.

— (1985) *Commodities and Capabilities*, Amsterdam: North-Holland.

— (1999) *Development as Freedom*, Oxford: Oxford University Press.

Senlis Council (2006) 'Landmark Journey of Afghan Farmers to the United

Kingdom', February, available at www.senliscouncil.net/modules/
events/london_farmers.

Shapiro, I. (1999) *Democratic Justice*, New Haven, CT: Yale University
Press.

Sher, G. (1987) *Desert*, Princeton, NJ: Princeton University Press.

Social Justice Policy Group (2007) *Breakthrough Britain: Ending the Costs
of Social Breakdown*, available at www.centreforsocialjustice.org.uk/
default.asp?pageRef=226.

Steiner, H. (1994) *An Essay on Rights*, Oxford: Blackwell.

— (1998) 'Choice and Circumstance' in A. Mason (ed.) *Ideals of Equality*,
Oxford: Blackwell.

Stewart, E. (2007) 'Figures Reveal High Cost of "Curing" Drug Addicts',
Guardian, 30 October, available at www.guardian.co.uk/politics/2007/
oct/30/immigrationpolicy.drugsandalcohol.

Strawson, G. (1998) 'Free Will' in E. Craig (ed.) *Routledge Encyclopaedia of
Philosophy*, London: Routledge.

Swift, A. (1999) 'Public Opinion and Political Philosophy', *Ethical Theory
and Practice* 2, 337–63.

Taylor-Gooby, P. (2004) 'The Work-Centred Welfare State' in A. Park *et al.*
British Social Attitudes: 21st Report, London: Sage.

— (2005) 'Attitudes to Social Welfare' in N. Pearce and W. Paxton (eds)
Social Justice: Building a Fairer Britain, London: IPPR.

Taylor-Gooby, P. and Hastie, C. (2002) 'Support for State Spending: Has
New Labour Got it Right?' in A. Park *et al. British Social Attitudes: 19th
Report*, London: Sage.

Taylor-Gooby, P. and Martin, R. (2008) 'Trends in Sympathy for the Poor'
in E. Clery *et al. British Social Attitudes: the 24th Report*, London: Sage.

Thaler, R. and Sunstein, C. (2008) *Nudge: Improving Decisions About
Health, Wealth, and Happiness*, New Haven, CT: Yale University Press.

Toynbee, P. and Walker, D. (2008) *Unjust Rewards: Exposing Greed and
Inequality in Britain Today*, London: Granta Books.

Treanor, J. and Jones, R. (2007) 'Banks Shoot Down IVA Rockets', *Guardian*,
30 January, available at www.guardian.co.uk/money/2007/jan/30/
creditanddebt.business.

US Census Bureau (2007) *Income, Poverty, and Health Insurance Coverage
in the United States*, available at www.census.gov/prod/2007pubs/
p60-233.pdf.

van Baal, P. *et al.* (2008) 'Lifetime Medical Costs of Obesity: Prevention

No Cure for Increasing Health Expenditure', *Public Library of Science Medicine* 5, e29.

van Parijs, P. (1995) *Real Freedom for All*, Oxford: Oxford University Press.

Webb, S. (2009) 'Government Masks the Real Problems in the Welfare System', 11 March, available at www.libdems.org.uk/home/welfare-reform-bill-2008-09-189468140;show.

White, S. (2003) *The Civic Minimum: On the Rights and Obligations of Economic Citizenship*, Oxford: Oxford University Press.

Willetts, D. (1992) *Modern Conservatism*, London: Penguin.

Williams, F. (1988) *Social Policy*, Cambridge: Polity.

Williams, M. (2000) 'The Uneasy Alliance of Group Representation and Deliberative Democracy' in W. Kymlicka and W. Norman (eds) *Citizenship in Diverse Societies*, Oxford: Oxford University Press.

Wolff, J. (1998) 'Fairness, Respect, and the Egalitarian Ethos', *Philosophy and Public Affairs* 27, 97–122.

— (2000) 'Beyond Responsibility', *Times Literary Supplement*, 5 May, 28–9.

— (2006) *Introduction to Political Philosophy (Second Edition)*, Oxford: Oxford University Press.

Wolff, J. and de-Shalit, A. (2007) *Disadvantage*, Oxford: Oxford University Press.

Womack, S. (2007) 'Brown Urged to Reform UK Welfare Policy', 6 November, available at www.telegraph.co.uk/news/newstopics/politics/labour/1568349/Brown-urged-to-reform-UK-welfare-policy.html.

Woodward, W. (2006) 'Cameron Promises UK Bill of Rights to Replace Human Rights Act', *Guardian*, 26 June, available at www.guardian.co.uk/politics/2006/jun/26/uk.humanrights.

Work and Pensions Select Committee (2007a) *Benefits Simplification: Volume I, Seventh Report of Session 2006–07*, available at www.publications.parliament.uk/pa/cm200607/cmselect/cmworpen/463/463i.pdf.

— (2007b) *Full Employment and World Class Skills: Responding to the Challenges, Eighth Report of Session 2006–07*, available at www.publications.parliament.uk/pa/cm200607/cmselect/cmworpen/939/939.pdf.

Young, I. M. (1996) 'Communication and the Other: Beyond Deliberative Democracy' in S. Benhabib (ed.) Democracy and Difference: Contesting the Boundaries of the Political, Princeton, NJ: Princeton University Press.

Index